Cover Design by Travis Pennington at
ProBookCovers

PUBLISHER'S NOTE
The publisher of this book neither agrees nor
disagrees with its content in some cases, and
instead remains neutral. The publisher does,
however, believe that the subject matter is of
utmost importance.

YAUPON PRESS

This work is to honor Martin and Louise Sonnenberg (nee Theophil), our parents. They cared superbly for my sister Sylvia and me and then sacrificed to save our lives out of the fascist nightmare, thus making this memoir possible.

I also dedicate this book to the children of the Orphanage Helenowek, in Poland, who were there not by their choice, and then scattered around the world, from end to end. They all suffered severe trauma and upheaval of and from the Holocaust. Many are no longer living, and others I am saddened not to have been able to include.

Acknowledgments

I thank all the people who have augmented my memory and supplied me with photographs, the sort of photographs I never kept, becoming discouraged after seeing houses smashed open during the war and the family photographs carried by the wind in dense clouds along the debris strewn-streets.

I thank **Bronek Cyngiser** for memories and the photographs, which he so blessedly kept.

I thank **Sylwia Sonnenberg** my sister for being with me and keeping the household while I was laboring on these memoirs.

I thank **Akiwa Brand** for allowing me to use his letters for the insertion of sad and moving memories.

I thank **all those** who contributed by being in my life, which has been so sadly exciting.

Note

I will use the term **Mentor** throughout the text to describe the function of those of the orphanage personnel whose responsibility it was to care for the group of children assigned to them day and night. They lived on the premises, as did all of the personnel.

INTRODUCTION

A number of people who survived the German occupation of Poland during WWII are still alive and scattered around the world. The personal history of every one of those people is woven in a series of unexpected events, tragic or fortunate encounters, fateful life decisions, and miraculous deliverances. Those people are not young anymore and if they have not published their memories by now, it is doubtful they ever will. Nevertheless, certainly, these testimonies are enormously important for recording history, for understanding human psychology and not least for purely human reasons. We want to know and should know about these perilous times and how people behaved in dramatic and often tragic circumstances under relentless and lasting danger. We want to know what we can expect from strangers, from people close to us and from ourselves. The more testimony about those times, the broader our knowledge of the world around us, the more profound is our understanding of it. We should not allow the facts to fade away into oblivion as the witnesses depart from us. It is also very important to leave a memorial to those who did not survive the terrible times; it is vital that they not be forgotten.

A TWO STEP JOURNEY TO HELL

By

Sven Sonnenberg

PART I

UNDER

FASCISM

I was born Sven Sonnenberg in 1931 in Grudziadz, Poland. My family home and business were located in Jablonowo, about 25 kilometers east of Grudziadz. This was less than twenty kilometers from the border of East Prussia from where the Germans mounted their invasion on that part of Poland in September 1939. In 1939, my family consisted of my father Martin, my mother Louise, my sister Sylvia and myself, age seven, at that time, and the narrator of this account. On the same premises lived my grandmother, Laura, and three uncles, Alfred, Magnus and Ari.

MY PARENTS SHORTLY AFTER
THEIR WEDDING

The family owned and operated a wholesale warehouse situated in the center of Jablonowo on a large piece of land. The property consisted of two multistory houses, and several utility buildings. This prosperous warehouse was a distribution center for the vicinity. Expansion was contemplated before the war's outbreak.

My family was a close–knit unit all working in the business at their assigned duties. My father was the accountant and salesman. My parents were very dedicated to each other, the feeling of mutual love between them permeated every single day as far back as I can remember.

Our family with a friend, who sits to the right. Father is standing. I am seven years old holding Sylvia, three.

They never argued. This feeling of being blessed, of having each other made any issue that could have come between them small and insignificant. Although my mother was a strict disciplinarian her love and care for us children was obvious and ever present. Her devotion to us made any punishment that she meted out for my misbehavior bearable and of lasting educational value. This is how I remember them. Unfortunately only very few photographs survived the holocaust years.

PRELUDE

My first year in school ended badly. I went into the recess of summer 1939 with turmoil in my seven-year-old head. Right from the start the beautifully embroidered Tyrolese shorts, my mother so insistently outfitted me with was trouble. The whole first grade and beyond had a field day. My first love, Sophie, a little playful blond, sneered at me mercilessly, but the end of my first-grade year was more serious and ominous. One day the teacher asked the children:

"Now, each of you tell me what do you have on the wall over your bed?"

The variety of things was not great, mostly crucifixes and the Virgin Mary.

"Sven, what do you have?"

I had the framed portrait of Marshal Smigly- Rydz (the supreme commander of the Polish Forces).

"Look children, a little Jew, and what a patriot!"

That has stayed with me to this day, and will forever. I understood right there that I was different and no matter what merit I might show I was basically flawed and there is no escape from that. From that point on, I tried to excel in whatever I was doing to diminish that flaw in the eyes of whoever I was with. Until one day, I did not give a damn anymore and I experienced a reversal. I saw the entire gentile world with a healthy dose of skepticism and no longer did things because I was viewed as a Jew.

In August during the school recess, exciting things were happening. The Polish army conducted maneuvers and mock battles in the surrounding countryside. A contingent of soldiers camped in our large yard, and slept in our utility buildings. To the utter dismay of my mother, I became uncontrollable. I would not eat her spinach, because I ate with the soldiers from their tins while sitting with them in a circle. The dark coarsely ground bread was such a delight after the white fluffy rolls. The soldiers let me do little chores around their equipment. Great times!

At home, the conversation was more and more about a possible war. My mother implored my father to leave Poland, to go to Switzerland, or anywhere out of the line of a possible German advance. Switzerland was most often discussed, because I think, they had some ties there. I knew they had business associates and friends. I myself was not too concerned; the mighty Polish army would protect us. Certainly, the parades through Main Street were impressive. The radio and the speeches were also very reassuring. "We will not let them have one button" (from their uniforms, apparently). "If they attack us we will be in Berlin in two weeks." And so, a busy summer passed, the soldiers were leaving and I was sad again.

I remember vividly the early morning of September 1, 1939. We children had just crawled into our parents' bed, which was allowed on that day, and the weather was shaping up—it would be bright. That was clearly visible through the window opposite the parental bed. Suddenly we heard rumblings as if a thunderstorm was approaching.

My father said not to worry—I was with them. I always was terrified by thunder and lightning. The rumbling got louder and suddenly a big explosion could be heard in our yard and two fair – size holes appeared in the window. A shrapnel fragment embedded itself in a piece of furniture. That is how W.W.II began for us.

My parents grabbed us and we ran into the basement. The basement was somewhat prepared, with sandbags in its windows, water containers and some towels to put over our mouths as a protection against a possible gas attack. Looking back now, it was all naive to the point of stupidity. I think it matched Poland's preparedness for war. Once the shelling stopped our family decided to pack a few things, on our horse-drawn freight wagons and run deeper into Poland. We were living about 20 kilometers from Germany's East Prussia. So we ran, for three days. The smell of fresh hay in the barns where we slept in the countryside comes back now every time I mow the grass.

After we had meandered around for three days, we realized that the Germans were everywhere. The only logical thing to do was to head back home. At home, the new instant owners of what for generations had been ours met us. These were the business tenants who rented store space in one of our houses. They declared themselves to be of German ancestry and became what was called Volksdeutche, which means ethnic Germans. Not Reichsdeutche—that was a better German. Still, a Volksdeutche was vastly superior to anyone other than a Reichsdeutche. These "ethnics" wore distinguishing armbands and were holier than thou. We were "put up" in one room in what was once our house. All our belongings and business assets were under the control of this ethnic family until further disposition by the new German military administration. In two weeks we learned that the territory would be made "Juden Frei" –free of Jews and we were packed into a special train with one suitcase per person on our journey, nobody knew where.

THE JOURNEY

This was an ordinary train ride, you might say. The compartments were full since all the Jewish families were crammed into a special car attached to a normally scheduled train. This car was shunted around a lot at several junction stations to be attached to other trains heading toward a destination only the Germans knew. I think there was only one car initially, because there were only a few Jewish families in Jablonowo, judging from the attendance at the synagogue where father took me on Saturdays. We finally arrived at a station named Dzialdowo. To say that we stepped out would not be correct. When the train stopped we saw soldiers alongside it holding sticks and waiting for the train to make a full stop. They then opened the doors and shouted " Raus, schnell, raus, raus Judishe schweine!" (Out, Jewish pigs). They handled their sticks so as to hit selected people and made everybody hurry to form what turned out to be a long column, four in a row. When that column was ready, the march began. Apparently many rail cars like ours were assembled into a purely Jewish train. We marched through what appeared to be a small dingy town and arrived at what looked like military barracks. The column stopped at an entrance, which turned into a fairly broad alley with a tall chain-link fence on both sides. Alongside each fence there were soldiers stationed every few yards, each with a horsewhip in his hand. Then their fun began. The commanding officer shouted:

"Run to the barracks, on the double!"

We started running, my parents on each side trying to shield my sister and me from the whip blows, which fell on us as frequently as the soldiers managed to bring their whips around. The commotion was huge. The sound of whips, the screams of people and the shouting of the Germans:

"Schneller, schneller!" (Faster, Faster)

At first, I was so terrified that I could not think of anything—the fear drowned all other emotion. The alley was between fifty and a hundred yards long. No lashes reached me as we proceeded because my father on my right side blocked them. I started to be concerned about Grandma who was one row behind us, and she was 80 years old then. I turned to see that my uncles were half carrying her, dragging her feet on the ground, terror on her face, but again the lashes fell on my three uncles, who managed to shield her perfectly. Finally we reached a building and ran in. It was getting dark; we could barely make out the interior. It was a large interior, certainly not a barracks, rather as if it had been a huge storehouse or maybe an empty stable for horses. On both sides along the walls were areas with a layer of straw on the ground framed by planks so as to form passageways in the middle along the vast interior. The space was filling up rapidly, families were grouping on the straw areas lying down, making the best arrangement with those of their meager belongings not lost during the running of the gauntlet.

I can't remember how long we were kept there, camping on the straw the whole time. This is where family clusters "organized "their everyday lives, including all functions except going to the open latrine behind the building. Only two vivid memories remain from this long, terrifying sequence of events. The next day a small group of Germans (at that time I was unable to distinguish

uniforms or services, they all were military of some sort)
came in, with one of them obviously being the boss, for
what looked like an inspection. He stopped at a place where
he could be heard by most and loudly announced:

> "These quarters were carefully prepared for your
> comfort. I want them kept clean. The passageways
> must be swept and free of even one stalk of straw. I
> do not want my soldiers to stumble and get hurt.
> Therefore severe punishment will follow any
> noncompliance."

We saw the punishment the next day. One bastard,
having found a straw, selected a young man from the group
near where he found it and whipped him unconscious.

Close to our family group, camped another large
family. There was a baby who started crying at some point,
and would not stop; we could not sleep because of that. The
baby carried on most of the next day. Toward evening the
mother spoke out loudly,

> "My baby is sick. Something is wrong. Please pass
> this down the line, is there a doctor somewhere. The
> baby has not peed for two days."

Sure enough, there was a doctor; I was very curious
and tried not to miss any detail. The doctor said that the

little guy needed an operation on his penis because of a blockage. The doctor obviously did not have what was necessary for that, but he performed the operation anyway with a pocketknife and improvised with whatever the neighboring clusters of people were able to find for him. The little guy urinated very soon and we could sleep again. Happiness reigned among our neighbors.

Somehow my parents protected me from the entire nasty goings on until our departure, which was, again, terrifying. I remember getting on the train under the blows of sticks wielded by the Germans. They obviously enjoyed herding us from place to place. From the safety of the compartment I saw a scene to be repeated many times in the future: The train platform from where people were driven into the wagons, German soldiers milling around, some closing the doors, and everywhere debris left on the ground, some purses, hats, pieces of garments and a body here or there. And so we set out to a destination unknown.

They unloaded us in Plock, a historic Polish city. A Ghetto was installed in its midtown area along the Wide Avenue (Ulica Szeroka) ringed by monuments of this city's splendid past. Cathedrals and churches and other places of historical significance sat all along the high banks of the Vistula River. With the onset of the extremely cold winter of 1940, life became harsh right away. The biggest problem was hunger. My father went out day after day trying to find some food for us. He sold little by little the few jewelry pieces my parents still had. Amazingly there were buyers. The problem was, where to get food for the money. The ghetto was a holding area for thousands of people without any normal economical activity. There were no jobs, no flow of supplies, and no stores. This semblance of an isolated mini-society was in a state of suspension and lingered from day to day, waiting for various ominous developments. The only civic organization existing and allowed to function was the "Gmina Zydowska" – the Jewish Council that passed German orders to the populace and attempted to distribute what meager supplies reached the ghetto from outside. It also organized the work contingents requested by the Germans and tried to implement all kinds of foul ordinances.

One day, in utter exasperation, my parents asked me to go outside the ghetto and buy some food. They agonized about it because it was very dangerous. Eventually they decided that I did not look all that Jewish and had a chance to pass as a Polish boy. Any Jew, if caught outside the ghetto with or without the Star of David armband could be shot. So, I went out of the ghetto. The store was only a block away, I got into the line and soon arrived at the counter.

"Two loaves of bread please and a quarter kilo of butter."

"Sure, but are you not a little Jew, by any chance?"

"No,"

"Well then, cross yourself."

To do that meant to take two fingers of the right hand and touch the forehead, left and right shoulders and belly in the right sequence. I did not know how to do that! This was a moment of terror I have never forgotten. I did not know what to do. Run? – Not possible. The store was too crowded. So, I stood there befuddled for a while.

"What is the hold up?" – shouts from behind.

"I think a little Jew has wiggled his way into the line here."

"Somebody get a policeman, I will hold him."

I was numb with terror. Suddenly an older woman pushed her way from behind until she was close to the counter and me. She spoke to the clerk.

"What is going on here? What do you want from

this little boy? Don't you see that he has been scared stiff by you and the crowd here?"

"What do you need, boy?"

"I....I wanted bread and a piece of butter."

"To me he speaks perfect Polish. Give him the bread and don't waste our time. I don't want to have to complain to my son about the inefficiency in this store."

"Yes, Ma'am..."

I would never know who that lady was. With my "purchase," I tried not to run home, but to walk casually on my shaky legs, my face paper white from the slowly subsiding numbing terror.

The pervasive every day hunger – that is what I remember most from the Plock ghetto. My father coming home in the evening with everything he had managed to get that day. He would set it out on the table and wait hunched over with sunken eyes, wait for mother to figure out what to do with it. That usually was our only meal for the day. We would go to bed with the pangs of hunger only slightly dulled. There was another worry my parents had that seems silly in retrospect. It was my education. They found a teacher, to prevent me from losing time. I wonder now if this was denial on their part or did they genuinely not comprehend what was happening?

I received one lasting lesson and that was not from my teacher. One day late in the afternoon there was a commotion in our enclosed little yard, a yard surrounded by high walls on all sides with one entrance from the street. I was playing with some kids when the gate opened and a young man of about 18 was thrown face down on the cobblestones. In the door were two German soldiers.

"Find yourself a place here, Jew"

"I am not a Jew. I was born a German. I am from Hanover. My name is Adler, please; I do not belong with these stinking Jews."

"You stink enough, and don't make more trouble, settle in."

Adler got up and tried to move toward the gate. When he did so, one of the soldiers took the rifle slung over his shoulders and struck him in the stomach with the butt. He doubled over. The gate slammed shut and we got a new inhabitant in our little world. From that moment on I saw Adler coming and going, always with his head high and contempt on his face for whoever was around. Only once did I hear him speak. Passing through the yard someone shouted to him.

"Hello man, where are you from?"

"You will address me Mister Adler and I have nothing to say to you, except that I am from Hanover and I do not belong here. I was born a German and I will die as a German."

People gossiped a little, but not much. It was said that he was from a mixed marriage. The Germans had strict rules of heritage by which they determined if one was Jewish or not. That incident taught me a lesson never ever to forget. Never try to claim that you are anything but a Jew. I would learn this later to an even greater degree when I found myself among the Poles. They were usually such pure Poles! Although born in Poland I was very impure. I have gotten a hint of that already in my first school year before the war.

Mister Adler had barely settled in when the Plock ghetto ended. One day there was an announcement by a German soldier with a loudspeaker from the middle of the yard.

"All Jews must pack and be ready for tomorrow's assembly in the street at daybreak. Only hand-carried luggage is allowed."

That message was repeated three or four times as the soldier turned to face all four sides of the yard. After the soldier left we had all afternoon and night to "pack". The streets were suddenly alive with people rushing in all directions in bewilderment, trying to find more information or trying to place some prized possession with someone with a lesser burden. One woman, on our floor, an always elegantly dressed neighbor, brought over a pair of beautiful cherry colored leather boots. The only trouble was, they were ladies boots on medium heels and not fitting my mother. She said to my mother: "Let your son put these on and you pack his small shoes. If we get separated and I cannot retrieve them, they are yours. I can't bring myself to leave them behind. They are brand-new and a present. Out of terrifying hours of that time I still remember the lady's face and my distress at being forced to put on those boots.

In the morning we were ready with our hand luggage and dressed in multiple layers of clothing. Everything we could possibly manage to, we put on. My parents were sitting on their beds, my mother holding my sister in her lap. I was sitting by the side of my father, all of us in total silence, our anxiety mounting by the minute.

Finally, we heard the troops entering the yard. The noise
was unmistakable. We jumped, ready for whatever might
be coming.

" Raus, schnell, raus!"

(Out, quickly, out)

As we entered the yard I saw Mister Adler fly out
the opposite stairway entrance, shouting. "I am a German, I
am a German." One of the soldiers dispatching people at
the door reached over and gave him a good whack over his
shoulders. Then he was swept away by the stream of people
and I never saw him again.

We assembled on the street in rows by families so
that the whole long street (it was called the Wide Avenue
and had a median of grass and two cobblestone lanes on
each side) was filled with people as far as one could see,
everyone with a heap of clothes on and small suitcases in
their hands. On the side-lanes, German soldiers of all kinds
of service units were busying themselves with maintaining
order in the column. We were standing there waiting for
who knows what. Toward the late afternoon older people
and the sick started fainting here and there. We heard calls
for water, but no water or food was delivered. The soldiers,
oblivious to the cries, kept patrolling alongside the column.

Later the word was passed that the Germans will forgo the transfer of the ghetto to a new location for a price. People should give up their valuables, and if they did the whole thing would be called off. The representatives of the ghetto Council went along the column to collect whatever the people threw into their baskets. When this was finished, I saw a group of soldiers appear from a side street. They all carried sticks. On command they fell upon the column, hitting left and right, and shouted.

" Nach hause, nach hause!"

(Go home, go home)

Evidently, there were a number of groups of Germans whose job this was, to run people off the street fast. In panic, our family ran to the nearest door. We went into a building, and from the safety of a room that appeared to be an empty one-time store, I looked out onto the street, and saw the by now all too familiar landscape. The area was strewn with all kinds of possessions, garments in pieces, packages, and here and there a body lying motionless. Two or three silhouettes sitting up and rocking slowly back and forth under the darkening sky, the Germans walking over the area, casually poking with their sticks at this or that item on the ground.

The next day was quiet. Nothing happened, and we camped in that storeroom as best as we could. The next day, at dawn, the whole assembly in the street was repeated. No one was surprised at the ruse the Germans had played on us with the valuables' collection. In mid-morning trucks came, stopping at intervals along one side of the column. The Germans then separated out sections of the column and directed that section toward a truck. Usually a chair or stool was placed at the back of the truck so that people had to climb up that unstable support. Leading to each truck was the familiar deployment of two rows of German soldiers with sticks. Then, there was more "fun". In front of us was a family with an obese man who could not get onto the truck. We waited as he kept falling off that chair under the blows of sticks. Finally the Germans ordered him to stop trying and step aside. The two rows of soldiers closed around the fat man, and the beating really began. The heavy man fell to the ground and tried to protect his face and head with his arms. The Germans kept hitting him as if competing to see who could deliver more blows. After a short while they stepped away to resume the driving of people onto the truck. On the ground, I saw what looked like a big bundle of rags, motionless, a big balding head stuck to it with a bloody, messed-up face turned toward me as we ran to that chair behind the truck and that now frightening piece of furniture. My father shielded me from the blows of the sticks.

After the truck was packed tight, it moved out. I do not remember a guard in the back with us. During this few hours drive we passed small villages where people had lined up at the roadside and threw food into the truck. Apparently these were ghettos, which were still in existence along our route. Eventually we ended up in Konskie, a dingy little place. From our stopping point we marched through the middle of town and there was total indifference on the faces of the Polish townspeople, as if our march was the commonest everyday occurrence. We passed through town uneventfully and settled into the march to our destination about twelve miles away. That is how we arrived in Drzewica, the last ghetto before the Jews were taken to the extermination camps, one of which was Treblinka.

Drzewica was the place we stayed for a while. My father cared for his own family, whereas my three uncles and Grandma formed the other part of the family. We got a single room, my uncles a corner of a now empty synagogue. About two thousand people were crammed into a small area in this tiny village with no fences or guards. The perimeter of the ghetto was not even marked *except* later when typhoid fever kept breaking out. At the first Jewish house on each street a poster would be placed:

"DANGER TYPHOID FEVER BEYOND THIS POINT."

The ghetto formed a mini society, with "rich" people, "middle-class" people and the destitute. The rich were somehow trading their possessions for food, and that trade moved across the magic invisible ghetto boundary line. The middle class people – artisans and service people – were somehow surviving. The poor and most newcomers to the place like us were starving. This group grew larger by the day. Soon, there was a routine horse-drawn wagon full of the bodies of those who had died from starvation departing every day from the village to the cemetery on the outskirts.

A distinct group was the Chassids. They ran a cheder (a religious school) and prayed incessantly. They tried to maintain a corner of the synagogue and constantly moved books in brown leather covers from one place to another they thought more secure. Their behavior antagonized the rest of the community, and we became especially angry with them during the outbreak of typhoid fever. They would not let a doctor near them, and most dangerously, would not follow the basic rules of hygiene and quarantine.

"If God wants me to die, I will, no matter what is done."

They opposed any action directed to contain the disease. They were also magnets for the German raiders, who came to town periodically. They would seek out a few Chassids and line them up and amuse themselves by testing the sharpness of their bayonets on the beards of those poor devotees of God. When finished, the Germans would argue among themselves whose was the better shave.

A SALVAGE PICTURE SHOWING THE GERMANS AMUSING THEMSELVES WITH HASSIDIMS

Drzewica was slowly starving. Amazingly, people were still preoccupied with trifles and holy rituals were adhered to as much as possible. I remember an older man sitting on the stone steps at the adjacent entrance to our house. He was cutting his fingernails and very methodically collected the shavings on a white cloth. Asked why, he said:

"Don't you know that there is a commandment that requires hair and any other bodily clippings to be properly disposed of?"

After that, I always wondered what I should properly do with my nail clippings.

Apart from the everyday mundane death scenes there were some more dramatic ones. There was a man who lived in an abandoned railway freight car not far from our one-room dwelling. I saw him going about alone; evidently he had no family. His loneliness and the fact that he had a rail car all to himself piqued my interest. One day I saw him sitting with his feet dangling out having a feast from goodies neatly placed on the floor of the car at the entrance. He ostentatiously drank and ate for everybody to see. Two days later I saw the death wagon come by and men carrying the body of the loner out to dump him on top of the already high heap of bodies. I was told that he had traded everything he had for food, ate it all and hung himself.

I have witnessed the slow starvation of my grandmother and uncles. Uncle Ari died of typhoid fever and was carried out with the daily death wagon ride. Uncle Alfred and Magnus starved to death and were one day also taken out to the outskirts cemetery. I was seeing them first getting thin, skeleton like, and then they would become bloated and grotesquely swollen. That is the last image of both of them I have retained. I do not know exactly how

Grandma died. One day I was told that she was not with us anymore.

The time came when rumors started that something big was going to happen, though nobody knew what. It was said among other things that the entire ghetto was to be sent somewhere. My life in the ghetto up to this point had been a strange mixture of feeling secure in the family and jolts of terror from the entire goings-on around me. Whenever there was something terrible happening in the streets I always was able to run to the relative safety of my family. Mom and Dad so far had managed to keep the most horrible things that were happening to others away from me. I felt somewhat alienated from other children because of my mixed parentage – my mother was German. No strong rejection, but the kids would call me a "JEKE". Since they saw me sometimes sitting on the steps in front of the house and sipping a cup of fake coffee, it became JEKE MIT A TOP KAVE. So, I was a jeke and that also stuck with me ever after. It reminds me of the famous orphan character from Sholem Aleichem.

"Mir is git, ich'bin a jusem,." (I have it good, I am an orphan,)
I can say, "Ich bin a jeke, mir is git."

I do not belong anywhere. Drifting alone through

space, a stranger in any groups of people no matter what its makeup. The feeling of not belonging anywhere deepened after my mother died a few years later.

Moritz of Opoczno

Opoczno was a drab little town in the middle of rural Poland about fifteen kilometers from Drzewica. In 1942 it was the seat of a German garrison for the district, with a few buildingsfit for the occupying military and civilian organizations. The surrounding little towns and villages had no German forces stationed there and were controlled from Opoczno by frequent forays. In between, the Germans entrusted the administration to the black-clad police recruited from Polish collaborators. Drzewica, as mentioned before, had no Germans stationed there, even during the existence of a Jewish ghetto in the years 1940 to 1942. There was no barbed wire outlining this ghetto's boundaries. It was known which was the last Jewish house on the central and side streets, and a Jew was not supposed to cross that unmarked line. If he did the consequences were dire. Inside the ghetto starvation was the order of the day, with no goods or human traffic crossing the "magic line".

I once witnessed the following scene: My family's dwelling in the ghetto was the last one on the "main" street before the line, and looking out the window I saw a girl about 15 coming from the "Aryan side" toward the Ghetto line. She had a large bowl in front of her, which she held with both arms outstretched since it was large like one used for kneading bread dough. She hurried to get across the line, and almost made it. A group of four young Polish men caught up with her, grabbed the bowl and overturned it. Out came a heap of potato peels. One of the men grabbed the girl by her long hair, and kneeing her in the back, pushed her over the line. The others laughed and made rude remarks, shouting: "That should teach you not to leave your Jewish place again!" Undoubtedly there were Poles who had given the girl the potato peels (cooked, they were a delicacy in those days). However, there were always those who willingly and voluntarily maintained a watch over the Jews to keep them where the Germans intended. Those locals who smuggled food into the ghetto ran the risk of denunciation by their own, and death. Many took that risk, and some, only some, are memorialized at Yad Vashem in the Avenue of the Righteous. By and large the ghetto was isolated with about 2000 sick and starving inhabitants crammed into a small area. Sporadic outbreaks of typhoid fever added to the terrible toll from starvation, and the isolation was made even more complete by the German scare propaganda.

The head of the commando unit stationed in Opoczno was named Moritz. He raided the district villages with German precision and regularity. Often, because of that German predictability our ghetto was forewarned of his arrival. To know often made a life or death difference, since there was a nasty ordinance in place that the streets should be clear when he arrived. One day, a sunny summer day, he came unexpectedly. His three military vehicles, each holding a few of his cohort, stopped in the middle of the town square. I was looking out the window and saw the people running to get off the street into the nearest buildings and away from town center, where the Germans were jumping out of their cars. The Germans hurried, with their guns leveled at whoever was still not out of their line of vision. The shooting that began immediately left a few bodies on the ground. I was mesmerized by one man who ran toward a fence in a zigzag pattern, one German shooting at him, loading his gun repeatedly, missing every time. Then, when the man got to the top of the fence and balanced there for a moment, the German aimed carefully. I did not hear the shot I expected. The man got over the fence while the German swore loudly, and started to pull at his gun breach. Unable to open it, he took his bayonet and with its handle tried to knock the gun open. He held the gun upright against the ground with his left hand, bent over, and swung at the breach with the bayonet, swearing all the time "Donnervetter, eine ferfluchte scheise." Before long all the shooting stopped, and from a corner of the half open window I saw what must have been Moritz standing in the middle of the circle of his helmeted troops. He was slender, not tall but carrying himself very upright. He did not have a rifle or machine gun but a pistol holster and brown gloves. He swung energetically around as if surveying the scene and then barked some order that I did not hear. The helmets started moving out in a widening circle.

At that point, fear started seeping into me; I slid to the floor corner of the room so as to be totally out of sight. I did not know what to do next, so I sat there motionless. My mother, after going to the door and locking it, took my baby sister and sat down under the window in the opposite corner with her in her lap. She signaled for silence with a finger at her lips. Soon we heard a commotion in the adjacent room. There was a locked door opposite the entrance of our single room which led to another dwelling that we knew was some kind of an administrative office with a telephone. I heard voices; among them was the loud commanding bark of what had to be Moritz.

Then there was silence. Shortly after, another set of noises became apparent under the window, sounds of footsteps as if a number of people had gathered. Then the wailing and crying started. This was interrupted by a loud guttural shout "Ruhe"(Silence). After a moment a male voice: "Herr, bitte, the ropes are so tight, it hurts terribly ". I heard crunching footsteps of a soldier's nailed boots. "Na, ja, das ist doch zu stramm." (Right, it is too tight). Some muffled sounds and after that, the man's voice: "Danke herr, danke."(Thank you, sir, thank you).

The wailing started again, but very subdued. I could not make out the words mixed with the faint moaning. Shortly after that there was the clatter typical of soldiers when they assemble. All the equipment they carried made a distinct noise of canteens dangling, boots grinding against the ground, et cetera. The sound of guns being loaded was unmistakable. The wailing became louder. Then, we heard "Feuer" and shots rang out. After a short while the commotion in the adjacent room started again. Moritz was at the telephone calling Opoczno, and his voice this time was sweet and gentle. He gave an account of the day's work.

"Liebling es war doch ein richtiges vergnugen." (Darling, it was really great fun).

After this he must have started eating his lunch, because whenever he spoke it was as if with a full mouth.

We did not dare move until we heard the departing German cars. I stood up and looked out the window, trembling. Horse drawn carts came close to the wall and assembled in a line. Men carried the bodies and piled them up in the wagons. After this was done and the carts departed, two men with rakes came and raked dirt beside the wall below the window. Only when everybody had left did I venture out to look. The soil under the window was freshly raked, but I could clearly see darker spots and here and there was what looked like a shiny ligament or a piece of flesh torn away by a bullet. That sight has never left me and is as fresh in my vision as if it had happened yesterday.

As mentioned before the ghetto was unguarded. One autumn day we woke to noises in the street, a big commotion and an announcement that we all were being sent to a larger ghetto. Consolidation. This time the ghetto was surrounded by a motley group of Germans and black-uniformed police with some other troops said to be Ukrainians. We were trapped. We were told to pack, one suitcase per person, and be ready for transport in the morning. This time, in the evening, my parents held a soul-searching and dramatic meeting to decide whether to go along. It had finally dawned on them that something was very fishy and they should not. I remember some of the conversation.

> Mother: "If we must die, I want us to be together."
> Father: "You cannot make such a decision for the children. We must save them. I will come out and join you when I can. We could raise suspicion now, if I disappear too. They might start looking for all of us. We cannot risk that."

They decided that my mother with both of us children would sneak out and Father would join us the following night, since he had learned of two groups being formed for transport. For this to succeed he had to find a "black-clad" policemen and bribe him to let us through. So, in the morning before dawn we sneaked past an "unseeing "black-uniformed policeman, and then hid in the forest for two or three days. Finally, we ventured out of the forest. With my mother holding us both by our hands, we walked toward the village. There came a peasant with his horse and carriage. "What are you doing here, Jews? All the rest have gone to the gas. You can dig yourself a grave here. Do you want a shovel"? He drove off laughing. As we got closer to the village we saw a cloud of feathers. That was the result of looting by the hordes of locals – ripping the feather bedding is a necessary step in the search for valuables. We waited outside for one night, and the next day we entered the desolate area that had been the ghetto. Devastation was everywhere – a hurricane would create a scene like this. Belongings and broken furniture lay in the streets, and many windows were smashed. My mother selected a half-caved in house – hopefully no one would claim this one for a while. We went in to hide there, from the elements, since the autumn weather was worsening. It was now November 1942.

Drzewica

Until the fall of 1942 we had been confined to the smaller of the two squares in the village of Drzewica. The larger square was adjacent beyond a row of houses. These houses divided Drzewica and made a barrier through the middle of the village. Opposite those houses there was a large church complex. The ghetto territory was enclosed around the smaller square. To one side right by the dividing row of houses that allowed a narrow passage between the two squares was the synagogue. Drzewica served as center for the surrounding countryside. The "Odpusty" (church fairs) were held on the church grounds and I would guess that the synagogue also served the needs of some nearby Jewish families from the smaller settlements before the war.

The house that Mother selected for our dwelling was tucked in the corner of the square with its back to the larger square and facing the synagogue. This house partially caved in looked like a heap of rubble from the outside. Beyond the debris inside we found a room intact with a window looking out toward the now empty and looted synagogue. The view was partially obstructed by beams and other parts of the house. It looked as if one corner had collapsed and wrapped itself around the front of what remained standing.

We settled into this room. From the possessions strewn around the ruins we were able to arrange relatively comfortable living quarters. For a stranger looking at the heap of rubble with the small portion still standing but partially obstructed by debris it would seem improbable that someone could live there. Of course, our settling there was largely by chance, but once there we felt that its appearance was perhaps what was needed for a reasonable "hiding" place. The problem now was how to sustain ourselves. The greatest danger came from the locals. Would they leave us alone or would they denounce us to the Germans and especially to the gendarmes or the SS outfits that passed sporadically through the village to make forays into suspected partisan strongholds? Drzewica now, as before the liquidation of the ghetto, was free of any German military presence. The Nowe Miasto gendarmerie outpost was twenty kilometers away, and Moritz with his outfit was in Opoczno, about fifteen kilometers away. Drzewica was free of Germans except for "actions" that were carried out after being precipitated by a variety of factors.

These actions or forays struck terror in us. Most of the time we had some warning because the Germans came in by two access roads to the village. Both led into the big square. There the Germans would make their base and the commotion of this gave us time to hurry into the adjacent woods before they fanned out into the village. We would spend the day or whatever time was necessary waiting until they left. We could tell by approaching the edge of woods close to the village. The actions mounted by the Germans usually lasted a few hours until their goals had been achieved, whatever they were. The danger to us was that some of the locals might point our ruin out and that would doom us.

The next worry was food. Hunger was our ever-present torture. I went out to forage into the fields for leftovers from the harvest. I dug out and collected everything that I could find, frozen or not. Carrots and potatoes were sometimes buried deep enough to be edible. One day I hit a bonanza. I found an abandoned flourmill, and the flour and grain I collected from crevices sustained us for a short while. Times became better when the crops began to ripen. I went out and collected (stole) much of what was needed to keep us from outright starvation. Our everyday hope was that father would come back, as was planned. That hope sustained mother, she was so sure that we would see him any day. That was not to be, but mother never lost hope although chances that we would see him again at all diminished with every passing month, the three of us marking days in fear and desperation, hoping for some change for the better. By this time we were approaching the winter of 1943, almost a year from the time of our escape from the ghetto.

What saved us was an event that occurred before the winter set in, quite some time after the ghetto liquidation. On the other side of the river a huge commotion started one day. Construction equipment arrived, and a lot of black uniformed Todd organization units. This organization named after General Todd had the mission of supporting troops by constructing roads, fortifications and whatever was necessary. This was their mission and concern, not chasing Jews or any other military/political pursuit. With typical German single-minded dedication to their narrow mission they went about their task to build barracks for young Polish conscripts in a work organization called "Junaki" – Young Men's Labor

Brigade. These young Polish men did all kinds of auxiliary work for the German war machine. They were rounded up in actions called " lapanka" (roundup) and given a choice, to be sent to Germany for slave labor or to "volunteer" for the Junaki organization and stay closer to home, doing work for the Germans out of their "free will." I think the Germans considered that arrangement more efficient.

When that camp started functioning and we continued to be pressed for food (my digger-gatherer activity barely allowed us to stay ahead of starvation), my mother said one day,

> "Children, I have to go there and see if I can get some work. Maybe they need some kitchen help."
> "But Mother..."
> "Sven, I have no choice, we will starve otherwise. These are Todd people maybe I will find some human soul there. I will tell them some story about how we are temporarily here waiting for our paperwork that is being processed to restore my rights as a pure German (a Reichsdeutche)."

So, my mother got a job as kitchen help in the Junaki work camp.

This had an immediate and huge benefit; it gave us food and it also confused the locals utterly as to our status. Now they saw my mother go to work every day in the German compound. I was a little bit more relaxed and did not scurry around like a hunted animal anymore. I ventured to go and watch the kids play a game called "palant"-something akin to baseball. I stood there on the side, a picture of shyness and poised to run at any signs of hostility. One boy much older than me, a lot of them were sixteen or older, moved in my direction and said,

"Hey, little Jew, catch that ball."

He threw the makeshift baseball in my direction, and I caught it nonchalantly with my left hand. His face went from a derisive smile to very serious.

"Do you want to try a game with us? I will put you on my team."

No doubt that I would try a game! I became a prized player. The team captains would draw lots to decide which team I would be on. I was proficient catching with my left-hand and that was a premium. I gained confidence and felt safe as long as I was in the company of these familiar boys. Being now more open on the "Aryan" side I had a chance for a bit of insight into the life of Polish society during the years of the German occupation. The days now passed in an effort to avoid dangerous situations and most importantly dangerous people.

The village and the surrounding countryside were teeming with partisan activity. There were many factions constantly feuding with each other. On the average there were two funerals a day in Drzewica as a result of assassinations carried out by rival units against each other. All I knew was to keep from crossing the path of any of those units. I was unable to distinguish between the Communists (AL), the Home army (AK) and the Nationalists (NSZ). At times some of them would behave so brazenly as to parade in prewar Polish military uniforms through the village. While none of them ever bothered us, danger nonetheless loomed everywhere.

There was a large farm/estate run for the Germans by Polish tenants. This is where I went when crops were ripening to dig out some new potatoes and look for anything else that was edible. One day a farmer who had no interest in protecting German property (or so it seemed) caught me. His fields were not even adjacent, but here he had caught a Jew obviously stealing German property, and my uncertain status notwithstanding, this should do me in. He tied me to his cart with a rope and started dragging me to the nearest German authority. Where would he find one close enough so that I would still be alive after being dragged like this? I did not know. The farmer was driving his horse and I ran behind the cart in terror, stumbling and wiggling trying to free myself. Eventually I was able to scrape the rope against the rough wood of the farm cart and break it. I ran into the nearby bushes and escaped. The bastard gave up looking for me after a while—the head start I had before he could stop the horse and get off the cart made the difference.

There was a brief period of heightened fear, and it was not directly from the Germans; in 1944 the Warsaw uprising took place. We watched the glowing sky over Warsaw in the distance, and after a while refugees from Warsaw started arriving in Drzewica. A number of people escaped the burning capital city that was being systematically dynamited house by house by German troops. People scattered in all directions and a number ended up in Drzewica. Some turned out to be nasty. City slickers—they tried to show off. Inevitably some got interested in my family trying to show how tough one ought to be with Jews. They started harassing me at every turn. What saved us and particularly me from harm were the tough local farm boys whose respect I had gained through games. Besides, they had their own animosity toward the so annoyingly arrogant city slickers. The importance of judging people by subtle or not so subtle clues was hammered into me by another memorable incident.

One day I went to meet Mom at the Junaki compound. Usually I waited near the main gate, out of sight though, at an abandoned shack. The windows of the shack were missing, and the part of the wall away from the compound was missing too. I would join Mom when she came out after she finished her shift. On that day I saw a girl about eighteen years old dressed in a lightweight black dress. The dress was short, showing her legs and it was snug around her breast, which being nicely outlined appeared very firm. Her face was handsome, but bore a strange expression of bewilderment and absence of mind. Her movements toward the gate were erratic, as if she was not sure of her purpose. She had a bag slung over her shoulder; the kind beggars sometimes have to hold things.

One of the Junaks was standing at the gate, and the girl asked if she could get some leftover food. The man said:

"Wait here, I will check."

He walked back into the compound and I saw him collecting some of the other young men and four Junaks came out of the gate. Seeing this, the girl started drifting toward the shack and I was able to pick up the conversation among them. The leader:

"We need a rope or something to tie the dress above her head. One of you, go get it."

One of the other men:

"Yeah… I saw her before, I am sure she is a mental, she will not know what happened."

The girl was moving around aimlessly. The men came toward the shack and corralled the girl there. One of the men pulled her dress up over her head; the other quickly tied it up with the rope. They pulled her panties down. The girl was moaning and thrashing around trying to free herself and it was now that for the first time I saw a naked girl. She was beautifully shaped. Her dress pulled up high over her breasts, conical shaped breasts, firm and tipped up. The men forced her down in a corner. At that moment there was a shout from the gate,

"Hey guys what are you doing there outside the compound?"

"Nothing Sarge, just having a smoke."

"Back inside, on the double."

Obviously, he could not see the girl inside the shack. The four men moved in a hurry toward the gate and the sergeant. Shaking, I went over and untied the rope; I saw her face close—the expression was of sheer terror. She was moaning and sobbing softly. I picked up her bag, she slung it over her shoulder and still sobbing she moved away without a word. I sat down with my face covered, devastated. Amongst all the horrors of that war this one episode has etched itself into my memory, so that, whenever I think back to the war that scene floats up every time. I resolved then and there to redouble my caution around humans, be they German or not.

Nonetheless, my curiosity about all kinds of trades brought me into contact with a local Polish cabinetmaker living with his family and working in his shop near our hiding place—the abandoned ruin. Cabinetmaker named Ramus. I would spend a lot of time in his shop helping with whatever he allowed me to do. He also gave us shelter if there was an unexpected raid, especially in winter when it would be difficult to hide in the forest. He did so matter-of-factly with a calm demeanor as if it was the most routine thing. He risked the destruction of his family if not worse by doing this and he knew it.

Soon the Russians were approaching and the situation changed dramatically. We heard the rumble of artillery in the distance. There was anticipation, anxiety about impending events. The German occupation was drawing to an end. In addition there was the assassination attempt on Hitler, which temporarily threw the Germans into some confusion. I remember front line soldiers marching westward through the village, bedraggled, foraging for food and ingratiatingly saying,

"Hitler kaput."

Suddenly the area was flooded with Wermacht troops from all kinds of units preparing to make a stand. We huddled in the deepest crevices of that building we had found, not daring to breathe loudly. One morning we saw two German soldiers searching, and eventually they came upon us. A tall sergeant yanked me out of a corner. "People here tell us that you are Jews. Are you?" Ugh ..... Ehhh .....

"You, boy, come with us to the major."

The major asked a few questions but his main

interest was to see if I spoke fluent German, which I did.

"You will be assigned to the sergeant, boy. We will give you some provisions now, and you report tomorrow at dawn to him. We have trenches to dig, and you will translate instructions to the locals who are already organized in work groups."

Some more bastards tried again. One day, while going busily about the trenches I saw a vehicle stop in the distance. Out came four or five black–clad Totenkopf SS (the skull insignia was their mark, placed on their caps). One of the trench diggers stopped and went over to the SS men and I saw him pointing in our direction. I could feel the blood draining out of my face. All one had to do was to point a finger and say "JUDE" to these guys. The sergeant, as if alerted by something, looked at my face.

"What is the matter?"

I barely came out with a whisper,

"SS."

He took one look and barked:

"Get behind me."

We inched toward the nearest structure. "Crawl into a hole and stay there until I come for you." I heard his boots crunching away in the direction of the SS men.

The Snow Storm

The approaching but still remote artillery rumblings became louder by the day. Depending on the wind direction some days the booms became more pronounced and then faded away again. I could feel the mounting apprehension and fear among the German soldiers. These were the troops designated to hold the line at Drzewica and the trench work was being accelerated. However dejected they were, they were still far from the state of those marching from the front through the village in a state of decline after the failed assassination attempt on Hitler, on 20 July 1944, by von Stauffenberg. At that time, their spirit was utterly broken and they looked for food handouts from the on-looking villagers, shouting "Hitler kaput!" I was looking at their march from a safe distance. Unfortunately, the Nazi regime survived and for a short time consolidated, and the deadly terror by all those Hitler goons, the SS, and others intensified. The German front soldiers, dispirited as they were, became a gloomy bunch caught in a vice between the advancing Russians at their front and the Gestapo, SS, military gendarmerie at their back and the Polish Resistance – the partisans, from all sides.

Once I became close to some of those individuals, especially to the Sergeant, and was treated decently even to the extent of my life having been saved and sheltered from the Nazi goons, it is inevitable for anyone with some human sensitivity to feel pity for their fate because those around me were either just tolerating me or helpful. On the other hand, one has to remember all the evil they have wrought on the World as tools of monsters. I have read a rather sizable book containing letters from German soldiers to their families throughout the war. What a joy and excitement it was when they first attacked Russia – a swell adventure, burning slashing, killing and marching forward. As the war progressed, the letters became gloomier by the week until they became reports from utter hell, with panicky fear of the Russians. So, one has to still keep in mind the German nation's propensity for war and to robbing, and cruelly enslaving their neighbors. It is in their genes. Cesar, 2000 years ago describes that. This is Caesar speaking, in his memoirs from that time, somehow miraculously preserved:

"...There is no disgrace in committing acts of brigandage so long as these are done outside the frontiers of the tribe; indeed this is regarded as good training for the young men and something which will prevent them from getting lazy..."

It looked that I either encountered some Germans being humans, and not Nazis or a bunch of ordinary family men forced into this horrible war. It is on record, that very sporadically one could find humanity amongst them, the more publicized and big one, but not the only one is Schindler. There was no violence or glaring mistreatment of the local Polish population by this unit. I credit the commanding officer the − Major for that. It seemed he was human and respected by his soldiers, his treatment of me testifies that he did not give a hoot about Nazi ideology; his easy ways with soldiers was so uncharacteristic compared to generally brutal Prussian officers.

Well then, there I was, in midst of that tension and activity of their preparation for resisting the Russians. It was toward the end of January, 1945. Three months later, the Nazi regime was dead, and I wondered what had happened to the Sergeant who had saved my life. The winter was severe everywhere in Poland, cold but not so severe around the village until the day the Major called me to say:

"Tomorrow, you make sure that you get some warm
clothes, and come to the compound after dark, and
see the Sergeant."

"Tomorrow" then, mother, with great apprehension and
worry, prepared whatever there was from rags we had, and
I, trusting that nothing dangerous awaited me from them
personally, but still fearful what it might be all about, went
to see the Sergeant in a cloudy dark and increasing cold
night. The weather that day started with a heavy overcast
sky, very light snow flurries getting heavier as night
approached. When I started out from our shelter toward
their compound, without any lighting around, I found the
way only because of the familiarity of the terrain. As I
arrived, the weather had worsened. The Sergeant and a
soldier were almost ready in their coats and caps with
earflaps, but overall not very suitable for what was coming.
The Sergeant said: "We have a meeting in the nearby
settlement, you will come with us."

We set out in the already late evening, the weather
worsened, with more snow and strong winds. It was not too
bad, however, until we left the buildings of our village and
moved into the open fields. A snowstorm started with
blinding drifts of snow driven by icy winds. I could not
hold my eyes open against the biting snow gusts.

The two soldiers walked side by side and the Sergeant told me to walk behind them to shelter me and at times he instructed me to hold onto his coat belt. And so we trudged along a road which was not yet covered with heavy snow, the fierce wind/swept it almost clean. The soldiers shielded their faces with one hand looking away from the almost level snow gusts and tried not to lose the trail in the dark. Occasionally, we passed a spotty forest growth, which made the snow gust abate a little.

Toward midnight, we arrived at a dwelling. On entering, we could see that it was a tavern, steamy, low kerosene lamp light, with many men talking and drinking. One bearded man among them got up, greeted the soldiers and offered a glass of vodka. I was ignored. The negotiations began. The bargain was thus: the Germans would transfer to the partisans an agreed number of rifles, grenades and ammunition in exchange for this partisans unit (apparently sizable), not to harass the Germans in the coming battle with the Russians, and if possible to help in an escape if things went bad for the Germans. I was simply interpreting what was said without much understanding of the entirety of the situation and wondering about a few things only afterward.

They are:

How did the Germans make the initial contact with the partisans?

How did the Germans know the location of that particular tavern?

What made the Germans confident that we would not be attacked right there on entering the settlement, although the weather was not conducive to any action whatsoever?

After the negotiations were over, we set out on our trip back to the village. It was now well past midnight, pitch dark and the snow gust were coming in from our right. By that time we had to deal with snowdrifts on the road and in places where the road vanished under the snow and the soldiers had to guess the direction. We made it back with the same arrangement, I holding at times onto the Sergeant's belt. I was back toward morning, still in the dark in our shelter, of the collapsed house, wet and half frozen my, mother pale green with worry.

Only well after the war, and after I reeducated myself out of the fog of Communism, I could guess what it was all about. The Polish underground had a number of opposing factions to each other. There were the communists, rather weak and ineffective in fighting the German war machine, called AL (Armia Ludowa – People's Army – big name only) there was a huge faction, numbering around two hundred thousand under arms (there were even higher estimates) called AK, Armia Krajowa – Home Army. Those were the political center. They were the ones effective in fighting the Germans with many restraints, however, because actions by them caused brutal retribution on civilians by the Nazis. They concentrated on sabotage, had occasional battles and the big one – the failed Warsaw uprising. Then there was the right wing nationalistic NSZ (Narodowe Sily Zbrojne – National Armed Forces) the second largest at about eighty thousand members. The NSZ feared Soviet occupation and were set to fight it after the Germans were defeated. After Stalingrad and Kursk they were sure the Germans lost the war and declared the Soviets to be enemy No.1. Poland fell under Soviet domination. The NSZ was accused of atrocities against other Polish underground organizations and hiding Jews and collaboration with the Gestapo. There is one clear and documented instance of their cooperation with Gestapo, and many anecdotal reports. After the communist rule under Soviet control took hold in Poland, NSZ and AK were severely persecuted and destroyed. The leadership of AK was killed or imprisoned, the regular members were pariahs under constant watch, but nevertheless allowed to enter society.

The mess in the Polish underground during the war was so profound that it is not possible to "sort it out without vodka," as the saying goes. All these "armies" had factions out of control, some good, some horrible, and that goes for the "centrist" AK. Some bastards in any of those organizations took to banditry and would rather be hunting Jews who were hiding than fight the Germans. As to NSZ, which declared to fight for free independent Poland, they were not good for the Jews as a whole they declared anti-Semitism officially. There is this Jewish question about any events, social, or political, "But is it good for the Jews?" The communists as it turned out were not good for the Jews either; maybe not gas chambers, but certainly swamps of Birobidzhan , uprooted from where they lived rounded up everywhere and sent to the "autonomous" unlivable region of the glorious Soviet Union. Plans and trains were ready. Only Stalin's death prevented the full implementation of that plan. How would Jews be found? Easy, they had it in their domestic passport Yevrei −Jew in Russian, close to 3

million. How would Jews be identified in Poland, Ah …
the Poles had a sixth sense, they prided themselves that
they were better at it than the Nazis. Does anyone wonder
why Israel's existence is so crucial? The morons of the
American Jewish Diaspora hope that there will be no Stalin
or Hitler for them. Well, something like that is in the
making already, blindness has no cure as yet.

I am sure that those negotiations were with a group
of NSZ. I do not know if anything happened further,
because the front approached quite rapidly, a short one-day
battle ensued in and around our village, and the Germans
were gone.

The end of the German presence came swiftly. One
day, in the morning, we heard all hell break loose. Heavy
guns were thundering and small arms-fire crackling. We
ran into the cellar and stayed there until all was quiet. After
we left the cellar I went for exploring with the throng of
people that came out of their hiding places also. The first
dead German soldier I saw was lying face down in the
middle of the street, his boots, belt and coat was gone. We
moved beyond the river where the fiercest fighting had
taken place. Bodies lay everywhere, on top of the trenches

as if killed in the process of trying to get out and run. Most of them stripped naked. The ones still partially in uniform were stripped before my eyes. Looters with armfuls of all kinds of German clothing were running toward home in fear that someone would stop them. I saw an elderly man pick up a handkerchief and put it on the exposed genitals of a soldier who lay on his back— an exception. Some wounds were terrible. One German had his skull partially blown off; little blood, just the exposed brain.

The throng of people was moving like a swarm of bees from one place of excitement to another. The Russian soldiers moved in-groups, rounding up hiding Germans. I went back to the Town Square and saw a lone German soldier wandering around in a daze. He kept muttering:

"Mein lieber Got, meine Frau, meine kinder" (Dear God, my wife, my children)

He repeated the phrase over and over. One of the Russian commanding officers pointed to a group of other Germans and told him to go there. In a little while two Russian soldiers marched the group toward the other side of the river. The spectators followed. The Germans were lined up at the edge of a trench and the executions started. One of the Germans, apparently only painfully wounded, fell to his knees and made a movement with his right hand as if asking for more shots, to be finished. The Russians turned around and left. The people fell upon the dead to strip them naked. Some were left in their long johns.

Mother decided to wait in Drzewica long enough for father to return and find us. The next day Russian soldiers came to the ruin where we lived and took me to their officer. My mother did not speak Polish.

"Who are you people?"

"We are Jews who escaped from the ghetto and have been hiding here in this ruin since then."

"You were pointed out to us by the locals here as having aided the Germans."

"When the Germans came to town we were pointed out to them as fugitive Jews and our hiding place disclosed. The Germans forced me to interpret for them. We were trying to survive."

That was the end of that. I established good relations with some of the Russian soldiers and was around them as much as I could be, fascinated with their equipment.

After the war we waited for my father in that cursed place, Drzewica. Out of 2000 people only 25 showed up to look for their relatives. Many more had taken the initiative to run and hide but like my father, they never came back. Two weeks passed and father did not show up, so mother decided to go to Lodz, a bigger city. The Jewish Council placed my sister and me in an orphanage in Helenowek, a suburb of Lodz, and gave mother a job in the kitchen as a cook. One day we traveled to our home in Jablonowo, where we found both our houses a heap of burned out bricks. All the rest of our business establishment was gone. Not an item from that extensive property was left, and the value left to us was a few acres of wasteland. The war was over. All that was left of our family was the three of us, mother, my sister and me, with the shabby rags on our backs our only possessions. Mother kept hoping that father was alive and would find us. She kept that hope to the end of her life. She died in 1949.

From here on I embarked on new a journey through another bewildering period of the Stalinist regime in Poland. My drifting alone through space continued, a stranger in any groups of people no matter what its makeup. The feeling of not belonging anywhere deepened as I moved along the new journey path.

Epilogue 1

After reading this remembrance, some people have asked me how the experience has changed me? And further, what were my emotions during these years of calamity? The first question is a very valid one and I will address it in detail below. The answer to the second question lies within the text and any reasonably sensitive and imaginative person can figure this one out. I will, however, describe one other episode from those hellish years that has been evoked by this question.

The Personal Changes.

I have often tried to imagine what and whom I would be if I did not experience all of these horrors and sustain the losses. I can see what I would have become by simply observing people who have been blessed with a normal sheltered life, affluence at home, a carefree youth, no war, no army service, college and then a smooth transition to a job, marriage after that, et cetera et cetera, so smug and confident, believing oneself to be virtually invincible. It is tempting to wish for that innocence, and yet I would no longer have within me the knowledge of human nature, the understanding of the level of evil to which a human can descend and the height of sacrifice and goodness of which man is capable. I have seen and experienced and learned the mechanics of human behavior in a laboratory that is impossible to duplicate in normal life. In short, I feel as if I have a kind of wisdom that is so much a part of me, it defines me and makes it impossible for me to imagine anything so remote as a life without horror. What is the price of that wisdom in the makeup of my character? Did I acquire a hatred for Germans, Poles, and Russians? Did I become permanently depressed or otherwise strange? The answer is complicated. I did not fall into a permanent state of bitterness or hate, although I'd be less than truthful if I did not admit to having those moments of hatred, especially against the Germans and powerless fury with an intensity that is much too well-earned. More often I am reminded of "The Godfather's" Don Corleone, who verbalized a principle which I had practiced by instinct all along: "Never hate your enemies, it will cloud your judgment." This understanding came to me with great ease. To avoid the bastards one meets in life and to fight them down, if necessary is just business. That spared me an all-consuming desire for revenge or the constant torment of remembering how profoundly I had been wronged. Indeed, I sometimes felt guilty that I did not join the magnificent Simon Wiesenthal in his pursuit of the Nazi perpetrators, but instead went on to build a "normal" life. The justifying rationalization is clearly that I was a mere youngster after the war, and unfit to do any such thing at the time. In a sense I have been walking through life as if in an altered state of being, wherein I am able to see a level of complexity that few around me can perceive or even imagine. I would argue that it has indeed made me "strange," and perhaps more so over the years. I am generally in a state of anxiety, always expecting or at least prepared for doom, with a predominantly pessimistic outlook. I am trusting, and friendly, but with a healthy dose of suspicion and caution. President Reagan had the right idea, but butchered the pronunciation of the famous Russian saying: "Dovieraj nu provieraj." (Trust, but verify). I seem to have been born with, or somehow developed, the perceptive ability to determine an individual's trustworthiness, and this ability has spared me many disappointments. My experiences have also made me brooding, and introverted yet very proactive in life situations. A well-known statesman once said, "When I close my eyes I see the map of the earth and the tumult of battle, the cries of suffering and death rising above it." I do not have to close my eyes; this image is with me all the time. It does not leave me, even in moments of exhilaration and joy, which are always muted and tinged with a dark underpinning. Indeed I have become essentially a sad person and that sadness became a scar that was impossible to conceal and made me appear strange to other people.

Having said all that, one might wonder if I would exchange this emotional burden for the innocence of an unscathed life. Perhaps the fact that I cannot imagine such a life speaks volumes in itself. If I met my more fortunate clone or some paralleled universe version of myself, I would no doubt consider him immature, naïve to a fault and view him with a tinge of contempt and affection, like an old soldier views a greenhorn recruit. I would wish to warn him, "Wake up, man, to the real world that surrounds you. Wake up to the beauty and the evil that are only a fraction of an inch away from one another." I cannot emphasize more strongly that the price of my sad wisdom is both horrible and unacceptable, and yet it is not possible to wish it away. Under no circumstances, would I knowingly set someone on a life course like mine to gain the sad wisdom I acquired. It truly would be akin to condemning a human

being to hell, hence the title of this narrative. The fantasy I often thought of would be to have some of the experiences I had, but with a happy ending. Nobody gets killed, the family reunites, the previous conditions of life restored. That would be an ideal lasting education, albeit still unspeakably harsh, to appreciate life and its complexities. Yet sadly, that is not possible and I am left to grieve for my lost family and my parents mostly, who were such magnificent human beings and yet God allowed them to perish in suffering. Who could be idiotic enough to believe: "What does not kill us, makes us stronger?"
Such fools "know not what they say."

The Emotions

Finding the words to convey an emotional experience seems almost impossible. Reading the greatest literary work describing emotional states still leaves even the sensitive and imaginative person without a true feeling of what the subject experienced. It was my intention in writing this to communicate events more than attempting a futile analysis and conveyance of my emotional turbulence. There is, however, one emotionally charged experience that floated to the forefront of my memory, as a result of this discussion.

We were playing the cherished "palant" game in Drzewica during the somewhat "looser" times of our hiding on the "Aryan" side, when a boy came running and shouting, "The Germans, the Germans, they are fanning out and surrounding the village!" Panic set in immediately. Some of the boys were teenagers and were always afraid of being caught up in one of the "lapanka" (roundup) and sent for slave labor to the Reich. I, of course, was in danger for my very life. We abandoned all implements and in a herd, without a moment's hesitation, started running toward the forest. Without much thinking I followed the leader and the throng. We scattered a bit and ran at the top of our speed toward the trees about a hundred yards or so away. Suddenly we heard the ominously characteristic crackling of submachine fire. Looking back, we saw a line of German soldiers advancing toward us. They were not catching up because they stopped to aim and fire, so their advance was not as fast and bit by bit we were leaving them behind. Nevertheless, the bullets were whistling around us, but I did not see anybody hit. That was one rare instant when I turned to God, and I remember putting my hands together for a brief moment in prayer, begging to be spared. That never happened again, not for myself anyway. I have prayed for others, but to no avail. My chest was heaving and my head flashing fragmentary horrible scenes of being doomed. In all this, there was an instinctive retainment of reason that often makes the difference between death and life. Once I heard the machine gun fire, I started weaving to thwart the aiming. Utterly exhausted and out of breath we reached the tree line. Once inside the forest we just looked back for a brief moment to see that the Germans were giving up the chase. The shooting stopped once the last of us reached the trees. The terror slowly subsided, but we all proceeded deeper into the forest as fast as we could, regaining our composure. The moment I felt safe, the worry and the feeling of helplessness about my mother and sister set in, and the overwhelming guilt of leaving them behind became unbearable. I tried to rationalize and console myself, reasoning that I would not have been of any help and also it was all so sudden, that it was an instinctive reaction. Nevertheless the hollowness in my stomach and fear for their safety would not leave me until I returned and found them shaken, but alive. It was just a flash raid again and they stayed in the ruin until the Germans left.

I wandered with some of the boys deep into the forest and came upon a small settlement where people spoke a strange dialect and never saw a German. They heard that there was a war somewhere, but did not know what that was all about. We lingered there for a day before heading back to our village. That experience—seeing those people as if from another world—utterly amazed me and I cannot forget their strangely different faces and the way they moved around their primitive huts doing their daily chores. Reading "The Painted Bird" by Kosinski years later and seeing the reaction of people to it: "Fantasy, could not be true." I answer their skepticism: "Do not tell me, I was there!" It is now with thorough understanding that I view films like "Deliverance." I often wonder what people feel and think when they see war stories like "Schindler's List" or other true depictions from the Holocaust or other wars. I could not watch "Schindler's List" when I saw an excerpt and the little boy in the transport. I was saying, "That was me there." I lived through it once, and I am not going to live through it again. It is at moments like that when my fury of helplessness and hatred flares up. Indeed, I must admit that what propels me in life is a well of spitefulness; I feel it in my chest. I want to thumb my nose at the human or heavenly (if there are any) generated forces that are trying to stomp me down and strike blows as if to see if they can knock me down for good. Even in retirement, after a lifetime of combat, these forces are not giving me a rest. Instead they struck one of the cruelest blows by taking my only joy in life: my beloved wife. We always expect the good outcome of human stories - the "Hollywood ending," where the lovers walk on the seashore, hand in hand, as the credits roll. It gives us a smidgen of hope that things can be right and maybe we, too, will have our share of happiness in the final reels of our own lives. The best I can offer in terms of hope is that I have survived to write this and I have won some battles. I am preparing myself for the ones yet to come; maybe I will win some in the future as I managed to do in the past.

******

My ghetto experiences come out of the recesses of my memory at the slightest stimulation. Even a seemingly remote association is enough. Reading Bruno Bettelheim's essay "Freedom from Ghetto Thinking" (Freud's Vienna & Other Essays, Bruno Bettelheim, Vintage Books a division of Random House, Inc. New York) easily brought it out and made me go back in time in an attempt to examine the state of my mind, and that of my parents' and fellow ghetto dwellers'. The central point of Mr. Bettelheim's thesis is

that Jews in the ghettos, by a long tradition maintained in
the Diaspora, acquired an attitude of total submission and
meekness, making the job of their extermination
astonishingly easy for the Germans. What was my state of
mind at that time, at age 11? I had no broad historic
knowledge of the Nazi movement or its stated goals, of
course. Fear, hunger and preoccupation with the day's
survival are the only things I remember. Mr. Bettelheim
considers it a given that even minimally educated Jews
must have known the truth about the Nazis. My parents
certainly were very well educated. Had they seriously
considered or talked about the ultimate consequences of
what the Germans were doing? Not that I remember. There
was disbelief about the possibility of mass extermination
even when someone hinted at it. "This is the twentieth
century, things like this are unthinkable," was the usual
consensus. What about events like the one described?
These were thought to be the excesses of a few devilish
types, like Moritz. If only the higher German authorities
might learn about it! To add confusion to Mr. Bettelheim's
argument that the eastern ghettos were bereft of those who
had had the initiative to leave the ghettos for the "past three
generations," I must point out: The ghettos established by
the Germans collected all those who were outside in the

gentile world like my parents. So, there were plenty of bright, modern, educated people in each of the ghettos, people who had freed themselves from the ghetto culture. What perhaps might be a plausible explanation is that these people hadn't had the time, willingness or opportunity to bond with the "masses", and become their leaders and turn them from "ghetto thinking."

The so-called masses of Jewish shopkeepers, shoe repairmen and tailors had no inkling of the world outside their narrow confines, much less about Hitler's writings and the global political goals of the Germans. The elite were naive, trusting, and "innocent". Sometimes people develop an instinct without too much theorizing or verbalizing they "feel" that something is out of kilter, and then act. Even for this to happen there needs to be leadership. Advocates of a certain course of action have to come forward. In Poland the instinct and the leadership were lacking. I grant this to Mr. Bettelheim. Suppose they were present, this instinct and leadership, what then, given the hostile surroundings where even the Poles were murdering each other across the political spectrum without any German encouragement? When I "lived" outside the ghetto later, I saw at least two funerals a day resulting from fights between different Polish partisan factions. Should a Jewish leadership (if there had been one) have attempted to organize armed resistance with that kind of outside conditions plus the aversion of the ghetto Jew to even looking at a gun? Theoretically it was possible. It has happened in a few places— with suicidal results. Should this have been the norm rather than the exception? Yes! I would, however, refrain from pinning blame on those poor, lost, bewildered, disoriented and leaderless souls who, dazed, went to the slaughter.

The ghetto people felt trapped on all sides. The murderous Germans! The hostility outside! For many who ventured to leave the ghetto if caught and delivered to the Germans faced instant death. Mr. Bettelheim cites the fact that once the Jews took up resistance there was help from the outside, like in the Warsaw uprising. That was far from even a hope in Drzewica. So, Mr. Bettelheim, I would not be so ready to attach blame to the poor masses of downtrodden ghetto dwellers. Besides, to organize resistance one needs not only leaders, but also some rudimentary vestiges of the defiant and combative attitudes that were totally lacking in those unhappy souls beaten down for generations. So the notion that something could have been done is purely theoretical and unrealistic given the circumstances of that period. Do I wish we had fought, run, hid, done anything but go on the transports? Definitely! What permeates me though is not shame, but regret that we did not fight.

To suggest, as Mr. Bettelheim does, that escape trough the Pripec marches was possible is a sheer fantasy. To ask a shopkeeper with a flock of small kids to pack up his family and head over the marshes into the Soviet Empire is completely unrealistic. Under Stalin the traditional murderous Russian anti–Semitism was simmering and Jewish leadership and culture was being destroyed. That much knowledge seeped through to the ghettos. The people who went to the Soviet Union were mostly communist political activists acutely aware that they would be shot by their competitors, the Nazis, Jew or not. Their Soviet political comrades shot many on arrival anyway.

I accept Mr. Bettelheim's concept of ghetto thinking. For it is within me to a large degree. I have to watch myself and be careful not to fall too easily into that mold, even now. My first instinct is always appeasement, even if it is obviously of very temporary effect. I act on my second impulse and fight only if I am cornered without an escape route. Not fighting, even in extreme circumstance, was the survival method for the Jews in the Diaspora for ages. This has conditioned us to ghetto thinking. However, the circumstances during W.W.II in the German occupied territories included the additional element of total entrapment would have been difficult for any national group even with the best attributes of resistance and fighting. So, let's leave the total undiminished blame on the murderous Germans and the schmaltzowniks (those Poles who hunted down Jews for profit)! It is also difficult to accept Mr. Bettelheim's assertion that:

> "German Jews (and those of Poland, too) permitted themselves to remain innocent, avoided eating from the tree of knowledge and remained ignorant of the nature of the enemy."

To lump the Jewish communities with those of Germany is not right. The Jews of other European countries had a right to expect protection, as had their gentile population. I clearly remember the Polish propaganda slogan just before the war's outbreak. "We will not let them have one button" (from their uniforms, apparently). Poland was smashed in 6 weeks, hardly much longer than the

Warsaw Ghetto uprising lasted. When almost every neighbor of Germany crumbled in short order there was shock and disbelief. How about those governments and elites, including the Polish, were they stupid and incompetent? Were they "innocent"; if not, then what were they? To expect from the Jews a superior foresight as to the outcome of the German onslaught is a bit much. I think one cannot escape the thought that things were much more complex than just the psychological makeup of the ghetto Jew.

So, we survived. I have to give this to Mr. Bettelheim, passivity was a sure death sentence. Many also perished by being betrayed, as I was, outside the ghetto. After the war we waited for my father in that cursed place, Drzewica. Out of 2000 people only 25 showed up to look for their relatives. Many more had taken the initiative to run and hide, but like my father they never came back. From here on, I embarked upon a new journey through another bewildering period of the Stalinist regime in Poland. My drifting alone through space continued. I am a stranger in any group of people no matter what its makeup. The feeling of not belonging anywhere deepened as I moved along the new journey's path.

Sven Sonnenberg
Winter 1997 Chapel Hill, NC, USA

PART II

UNDER

COMMUNISM

Introduction to Part II

The following narrative is an account of a twenty-three-year journey through Polish Communism. It was a very "mild" experience compared to the horror millions have gone through. There are a few reasons for such a "mild" passage, and perhaps of greatest importance is the fact that it took place in post-WWII Poland. The other reasons will hopefully be obvious as one goes through the pages. For the reader to fully realize the enormity of the crimes against humanity committed by communism I must make reference to the hair- raising account given in

THE BLACK BOOK OF COMMUNISM,
Harvard University Press, Cambridge, Massachusetts.

Unfortunately, the facts of these crimes are receding in the collective memory thus preparing the world for a repetition or for another bloody experiment concocted by "well-wishers".

Poland's experience under the Soviet boot was a somewhat unique compared to the rest of the Soviet block.

Not without reason was it called the best barrack in the Soviet Concentration Camp: "We will do the concentration and the people will do the camping." First, Poland was historically fiercely anti-communist and anti Soviet. The Poles, fought the Soviets after WWI in brutal battles, the national memory of that has not faded at all and the Polish nation is known for mass emotional outbursts; it has happened a few times in their history. Secondly, Poland belonged to the west, culturally, and the Byzantine machinations and docile submissiveness seen in the Russian empire were absent in Poland. Therefore, communism had to take a cunning and cautious approach to subdue that nation. Mild non-conformity was tolerated well into the postwar years (one had to be careful though, as shown later). The peasantry remained a land-owning class, which was unthinkable in the Soviet Union. The process of shackling the nation and eliminating academic freedoms and private ownership took some time. The other element of enormous importance was the Catholic Church. It had a stranglehold on prewar social life in Poland and became a difficult opponent. The Poles, in defiance, rallied to the church creating a mass opposition, ostensibly non-political, and completely religious but nevertheless an opposition.

How then did the average person behave and go about everyday life? I can compare this to a typical scene of a police arrest, where the subject resists the cuffs, but not too strongly, so as not to be accused of resisting the policemen. A half- hearted and expedient conformity had set in. People had to eat and care for their families and somehow progress in life. The bold ones, who actively opposed communization, were jailed, murdered, or sent to exile in the Soviets Union, preferably surreptitiously, out of the public eye. People suddenly disappeared without a trace. That happened to my wife's father. After unwisely making an anti-Soviet comment at work he was taken out of his workplace and disappeared. One day the family found him at their doorstep paralyzed from a stroke. When he had that stroke in jail, the jailers took him out and dumped him on the pavement. A merciful passerby finally put him on a train home. From the station he then dragged and rolled himself to the fence gate of his home. He was unable to walk.

Who then were the people doing all that dirty work? Plenty of those were available. The first to mention were the ideologues brought in on the heels of the Soviet armies. Unfortunately, some were Jews and a few attained highly visible and powerful positions. These people were of a special brand. They hypocritically denied their Jewishness—they were internationalists. According to the theory, nationhood should eventually disappear. On an individual basis these people were fairly "decent." What made them into monsters was the notion that "The goal justifies the means." Their actions tainted the Jewish shopkeeper, the artisan, the engineer, and the doctor and gave fodder to anti-Semitism. The somewhat satisfying irony was that they did not consider themselves Jews, and a further irony of historical proportions was the fact that they were later discarded by their beloved communism for reasons of political expediency in power struggles and declared enemies, because they were Jews—discarded like used-up implements.

It is easy to predict that the same fate awaits the left wing Jewish luminaries in this society once they achieve their goal of leftist rule. They will be pushed out and probably destroyed by other ethnic groups whose feeling of separateness and grievances they, the **luminaries, have whipped up into frenzy. This was and is their strategy, to affect a left wing-shift in this society by agitation.**

A good illustration of the character and morality of
the communist elite in Poland would have been one of our
supposedly very friendly acquaintances, Mrs. Gefon. She
was from the described milieu above, a lifelong communist
and a very decent lady. Yet when our five-year-old Jack
was very sick and we asked her to obtain a specific
medication for him through her relatives in France, she
inquired of her comrades if we were sufficiently loyal for
her to do it. We never got the medicine.

The second group was that of the prewar
communists in Poland and the far-left. They were fairly
numerous before the war, but they were a minority never
able to play a significant role in Polish national life. They
were now salivating at the trough; a trough initially
guarded by Soviet troops and—were they ever eager! The
third group was the opportunists and the lumpenproletariat
(a universally accepted German term for the dregs of
society from which Hitler and Stalin recruited their
henchmen). So if one kept one's head down and was
extremely careful one would survive if lucky enough not to
inadvertently get caught in some troublesome situation, and
such situations were plentiful at the time.

Where did the author of this memoir fit in that social kaleidoscope? To find out, you need to turn the pages of this narrative; I hope it will be an educational experience.

After submitting this narrative to the scrutiny of some of my friends, I was told that the last part and especially the final Epilogue that follows this part of the book sounds like extreme right wing ranting. Surprisingly, this was also the opinion of Joe, who reminded me of some terrible events that took place during our times together under extreme left-wing rule in Poland, and he supplied a short narrative and corrections for this writing. Tom, my editor, expressed the same opinion. I value Tom highly and want to listen and consider his opinions apart from totally submitting to his literary expertise. After reviewing the text many times over and doing some soul-searching, I came to make the following suggestion: The sensitive reader might want to skip the Final Epilogue. Neither Joe nor I could be called right-wingers; we are equally leery of the left and the extreme right. I have tried to magnify this by the discussion of the Taguchi principle in the last part of the Epilogue. The emphasis on the left is because I perceive it as a "Clear and Present Danger". The right does not have the sophistication and talent available; it is crude and unappealing to the compassionate soul. The left, however, is highly talented and has one tool in its arsenal, which has proven immensely effective, and that is an appeal to blind short-term compassion and to one of the strongest human impulses —envy. That is why class warfare is the first tool they always grab.

My decision not to modify that Epilogue, or maybe only slightly, is prompted by the experience I have had, and which is ongoing, with a walking companion who is a fair representative of the liberal elite in the US today, highly educated and well read, with a left-wing family tradition. Knowing the futility of meritorious discussions with a believer, I tried to avoid political discussions and interpretations of current events with her. Repeatedly and unavoidably, I was drawn into these and had to respond, and respond I did. That resulted at one time, in a half-year interruption of our daily walks and a state in which we were, to each other, incommunicado. We have resumed the walks now and of course the discussions. There is no point in these, but for me it is a confirmation of the dangers I feel and see. Initially the arguments back and forth were ostensibly based on logic, but recently I got a declaration:

"I am a socialist."

I listened after that to a long explanation as to why communism can never happen here in the US.

"Why are you so worked up about communism? Stalinism was a horrible distortion; if Lenin had lived then things would have been very different, and do not knock the Chinese so much. They have gone through an inevitable historical phase and look at their achievements now."

The dangers are from the relentless push to the left of course; it does not have to be Stalinism or Pol Pot, a stagnant, bureaucratic, shackled nation eventually rendering content zombies is sufficiently frightening to me. My response to my walking companion was:

"Communism is cancer; Socialism is Alzheimer's, my congratulations to you for making a wise choice."

My concern is for the last remaining engine of humanity's progress, which is the US of A. My walking companion, who I believe, is representative of a large segment of the educated elite, wants to gum up that engine by putting sugar into the gas tank (a favored means of sabotaging German military trucks during WWII). In the meantime, she is unabashedly enjoying an affluent suburban life like all her sizable circle of friends in my neighborhood who think alike, affluence brought about by that horrible entity, Capitalism. She is comfortable and would like not to give that affluence up, but others should, for the benefit of humankind in the **global sense**.

The Capitalist engine needs vigilant watching, of course, for things that might go wrong. Every engineer knows that: "Things left to themselves will go from bad to worse."

Under Communism
The Beginning

Around June-July 1945

The war was over and the everyday tension of
having to be alert every moment, night or day, vanished.
The fear of not surviving to the next day was suddenly
supplanted by the question, "what now." Mother decided to
stay in Drzewica for a while with the hope that father
would find us. Almost every day or so a surviving human
wreck from the original ghetto arrived in the village,
hoping to find some relatives. They stayed a few days and
after futile inquiries moved on. We asked everyone about
our father, but we only found two guys who said that they
had seen our father trying to escape from the transport and
that he had been shot by a German guard. Their tale was a
bit fuzzy and our mother did not believe that it could be
true anyway. So we kept waiting until no more people
showed up. In total we counted about twenty from a
population of over two thousand in the original ghetto. A
few, no more than five, survived locally, hidden by Poles in
the surrounding villages. This then, perhaps, is a good

statistical indication of how many survived overall in Poland, because the first instinct was to come back to the village and try to find some trace of family or friends. It means a survival rate far below 1%.

One day we found ourselves again all alone, the sole remnants of the ghetto and no sign of father. It was time to move on. With our bundles of belongings, which were tattered clothing mostly, and some food we hitched a ride to the industrial city of Lodz. We were told that there was a Jewish help organization there. When we found the place, we could easily guess that some important activity was going on in that building. There was a multitude of people coming and going and some just standing near a large gate leading into the yard. The walls on both sides of the vaulted gate entrance were plastered with messages photographs and pleas for information about family members. We looked at these for a while, but the chances that our father had posted something there were nil. We registered and were given some money and a place to stay in a loft on the top floor of a tall building. We shared these quarters with another family. The feelings I remember were those of curiosity and strangeness. The street noises of the big city and the confinement created by the tall buildings

filled me with unease. The smell of cooked food coming
through the open window was all-pervasive. Although the
life threatening dangers were gone, I still felt restricted.
There were no forests to run to, no fields of tall growth to
dive into if need be. The terrain was unfamiliar with so
much to learn about the new environment, anxiety ran high,
but I was not in fear for my life anymore.

After a few days we were taken to a suburb of Lodz,
a place called Helenowek. This was a well-known prewar
orphanage compound. It had gained notoriety because of a
flamboyant Jewish Commitee member, a Mr. Rumkowski,
who took a special interest in its running. He solicited
funds for maintaining it from wealthy Jewish members of
the prewar Jewish community in Lodz. Using imaginative
stratagems he got enough money to furnish the compound
nicely. There were three houses that survived the war intact
as well as all the adjacent utility buildings and a fairly large
greenhouse with a nearby orchard. The third house, the
smallest, burned down later and only the concrete
foundation remained; it was never rebuilt. In addition to the
principal buildings, which housed the children and
personnel quarters, there were all the elements of a farm,
with horses, cows and pigs, a rather large greenhouse and a

number of smaller auxiliary buildings. As legend has it, Rumkowski, when he brought in prospective donors to present his accomplishments, would pick out the ugly kids and hide them away. After the war in 1945 the Jewish Committee ran all this. The funds came from America through the Joint (a Jewish help organization) and some came from the Polish state. My mother was given a job in the kitchen and a room for herself. We, the children, were incorporated into the orphanage community and assigned to our respective age groups.

IN THE ORPHANAGE

I have a lasting impression is of the first dinner in a rather small room. Close to thirty children were seated

along two tables. I was led in and given a place at the end
of one of the tables. I wore my best outfit, one which
mother had laboriously sewn together with great pride. It
was a nice beige jacket and matching shorts. I sat down in a
deafening noise of kids screaming their lungs out. The
commotion and noise abated a little bit when the food was
brought in and everyone out of curiosity was trying to get
high above the table to see what it was. Amidst riotous
commotion the food was dished out onto the plates. Once
this was done the kids started eating. The ensuing quiet did
not last long; one kid took a spoonful of mashed potatoes
and slapped it into the face of the kid sitting opposite. That
started a general shooting melee. My precious beige outfit
was hit several times with red beet mush. It came out of
that dinner a total ruin. There was a plump, red haired, very
freckled girl sitting at the head of the table. At her back was
a cast-iron heater below the window protruding sharp
ridges. In the commotion she stood up aiming with her
spoon at somebody. In the meantime another kid moved her
chair, and she sat down and hit her head on one of those
ridges. Her scalp was split, blood started pouring and the
dinner ended with the kids quietly sneaking out of the
room. That very night my first real shoes in almost three
years—I was given them while still in Lodz—were stolen

from under my bed. That was our beginning in Helenowek, about which a number of people have written in later years.

The mayhem did not last long. A new principal or director, Mrs. Maria Fajngold, was brought in. She faced every situation with calm, unlike the other mentors who became hysterical with frustration. She would pick the worst offender and without raising her voice would say,

> "Robert, if you go on like this, you will be too tired to go to the movies this Saturday. You will have to rest, at home, and the other kids will go without you."

That usually took care of Robert. She instituted the so-called "children's self rule." This is an old concept in educational systems, but few educators have the patience, seriousness and talent to make it work. Looking back it seems that her personality carried the day. She was a tall woman, robustly built, but not heavy, handsome with pitch-black hair and warm brown eyes. She never raised her voice or used physical discipline, although she could easily overpower even a fairly large youngster. She always found a calm way to resolve a troubling situation. The children's council was democratically elected and all-important matters like discipline, projects and other matters were debated and decided with gentle guidance and not much interference from Mrs. Maria. She put a vision before us in a few simple words,

> "Children, we need to make up for lost time and work hard to prepare ourselves for life. Those of you who were less damaged by this horrible war have an obligation to help others not as able to get on with school, homework and everyday activities."

Her quiet, never dour, matter-of-fact bearing resonated with kids who generally were from middleclass homes. Some remembered the culture of learning and striving from their long vanished homes; essentially we were good material. She always listened attentively to any kid and was never dismissive. We could see that she took the matter of our concerns with genuine seriousness. In short we were all hers. There is no question that Mrs. Falkowska (Formerly Mrs. Fajngold, as will be explained) by the force of her personality, created a unique milieu, which is rare in the annals of pedagogy.

MARIA FALKOWSKA

She created a place where discipline was imposed by the children themselves and motivation for learning and excelling in artistic, housekeeping and sports activities was high. She attracted a lot of attention and help from the outside world and created an attractive and highly stimulating environment for the children. The care was superb, the discipline and standards to strive for were demanding. Corporal punishment was simply unthinkable. And these were the old days when it was the means of first resort. It was not needed; there was peer pressure for proper behavior and any misdeeds were dealt with without smacking. Often the offending kid would rather have gotten smacked on the head than stand in shame before his group or be deprived of going to a movie. In the first years she also brought in a lot of Jewish culture, but that faded out for a number of reasons not the least being the pressure from the Party to assimilate into Polishness. Most of us, her children, kept a very close relationship with her, way into our adult lives, even in retirement and from abroad. Mrs. Falkowska died in 1998 at the age of 92. Her mental acuity was amazing and she was physically active, living alone and caring for herself. One day a friend who was supposed to visit could not get a response at her door. She summoned Jacob (mentioned later), who had the key, and they found her dead by the bathtub.

From time to time trouble erupted with new arrivals. These were kids, survivors of the Holocaust, collected and brought in by special teams roaming the country and looking into all conceivable places. Shreds of information obtained from a great variety of sources led them to farmers, monasteries, and hiding places in forests. I vividly remember three arrivals. One was a kid from a disbanded partisan unit. His name was Stolin. Of course for us he became Stalin. We had quite some fun with this:

"Hey Stalin, who gave you that black eye?"

This was tolerated until the arrival of a new Mentor, Ms. Maria Milstein. The Marias proliferated fast because the communist Party and the state urged all Jews to polonize their names. This was a stupid and hypocritical action promoted by the then first secretary Gomulka. Some people naively went along in an attempt to avoid the virulent anti-Semitism (permeating the Polish nation), and the more Christian-sounding the name the better. According to the teachings of the great social scientist comrade Stalin, nationhood was defined in one of his "scientific" writings and one of the conditions for a group of people to be a nation was territorial separateness (oh… what wisdom!). Of course under these rules Jews did not qualify at all and they should disappear and melt into the Polish nation.

Nevertheless, the Party and state kept files on who was a Jew by heritage, and that went generations back. They boasted in 1968, during the times of trouble, that they did this much more thoroughly than Nazi Germany had ever dreamed of. When the time came they used it ruthlessly against us, Polish name or not. But this was just

the beginning and our principal changed her name to
Falkowska. With that her conversion to sublime Polishness
was completed. Maria Falkowska, the former Maria
Fajngold, was not a Party member, but the newly installed
Mentor Maria Milstein was. And that was the end of us
running around and having fun with our own little Stalin.
The ideological noose started tightening around us.

Ms. Milstein was a lifelong communist. [See Addendum B] She was a tall, rather skinny spinster who wore round
glasses a la Trotsky. Her black hair was tied back in a short
tail with a band behind her oddly shaped head. She walked
with a slight stoop and with a serious and purposeful
expression on her face. She never smiled; we could not
make her smile under any circumstances. Slowly, bit-by-
bit, we learned some of her life story. As was often the case
with the communist activists, she came from a well-to-do
Jewish family, rebelled and joined the communist
movement very young. She devoted her life completely to
that movement, suffering deprivation and jail for her
beloved ideals. In 1939, before the German onslaught she
ran to her beloved Soviet Union, where else? She was
lucky not to be shot on the spot like many of her comrades
— they being tainted comrades — on crossing the border

into the empire and she survived the war there deep inside the country. In short she was an ardent devotee, more ardent than most can become. In other aspects, she was reasonable and very caring about the children under her supervision. We quite easily adapted to her and even with our childish intolerance to her uncommon appearance, we started to rely on her everyday wisdom and help with school. Milstein however, had a specific mission. Her life was absolutely devoted to spreading and solidifying communism, nothing else mattered. Here she had a perfect opportunity to turn kids into fighters for her clearly religious-like cause and send them out into the world to build communism. She took to the mission with zeal.

MARIA MILSTEIN

Leaving Ms. Milstein for a moment, we need to go back to the two other arrivals, at the orphanage!

One day three Russian officers arrived and went to see our principal. The news spread fast through our community. The curious thing was that one of the three guys seemed so young. That was Misha, the "son" of the battalion. An orphaned Jewish kid found by the westward marching Red Army in a burned-out village where all the Jewish inhabitants had been killed. The Russians took him into their unit, made proper military outfits for him and called him their "battalion's son." The other two, a captain and a lieutenant asked the director to take Misha into the orphanage. Their campaign was over and he had to start a normal life and school, and so we got him, a spoiled rotten, know–all youngster a war hero with medals. That was a tough nut to crack for Mrs. Maria Falkowska and also for us, the Children's Council.

Misha never became what one would call a normal kid even by the somewhat loose understanding of normal. Most of us were severely traumatized and damaged. Strangeness reigned among us, but Misha was beyond the pale. He would suddenly put his hands against his temples, sit there for a while and then become restless and franticly active, sometimes challenging others. We understood that horrible memories must have been welling up in him. He never told us what those were. None of us did talk much about our war experiences. When asked, we would answer in monosyllables. Misha disappeared one day without a trace and without finishing high school. I never heard of him again, unlike the other kids who have kept track of each other to this day.

The third memorable arrival was that of the brothers Cyngiser, Baruch (Bronek) and his older brother Janek (Ichack). We were told that it was difficult to bring them in since they kept escaping en route to the orphanage. They were found in a village having survived the war in dugouts in the forest, evading Germans and Poles, who would hunt Jews for a reward. Their ordeal is described in a collection of stories under the title "Dark Year... Dark Years." They were both small in stature but strong and very active in exploring the lay of the land. They were mostly unresponsive when approached, displaying mistrust. One had the impression of wildness about them especially about Bronek. Kippling's story of the wolf boy comes to mind. Slowly, very slowly they did integrate and stop saying that they did not want to be Jews. Bronek became successful in school and in life and my best friend. Our friendship strengthened as we aged. Janek on the other hand could not adapt fully. He led a low-grade, difficult life and died young.

There are so many to remember and I wish I had the talent to bring them all to live, which regrettably is not possible and not only because of lack of talent. There was however another arrival that became part of Bronek's life and mine to some extent and that was Akiwa Brand. The first remarkable thing about Akiwa was that a good portion of his skull was missing. A silver plate had been implanted and if one looked close, one could see the skin pulsating on the side of his head where the metal met the bone. He was known for his restlessness and the intensity with which he did everything. He was a very good student. After the orphanage Akiwa had a difficult life, although he worked at a profession and later, after leaving Poland, became a chief engineer in the merchant marine. The best thing for me to do here is to give the narrative over to Akiwa, who wrote to me on occasion and I will pick out fragments from his sometimes-long letters. The bond that had developed between many of these children endured over continents and over half a century and is stronger even today. We were a big family. Here is Akiwa speaking:

The curse of my life is that I was born a Jew.
In 1944 the Russian army of the Belarus Front
liberated Wilno and I started grazing a herd of
cows and sheep. I roamed the surrounding fields
and hills until 1946. Other children were going to
school, but I was a cowherd. Two facts from
between 1944 to1946 are significant. When I fell
from a horse and busted my skull no hospital would
help me. According to the prevailing habit during
this war, the very seriously injured and the slightly
injured got no attention. Mr. Zborowiecki did not
allow them to finish me off and drove me in his
horse drawn wagon from hospital to hospital.
Zborowiecki was an engineer educated in
Petersburg and spoke perfect Russian. He would
not give up and finally past midnight he found a
place, a Russian Military Hospital where they did
the operation.
The other things I remember were hunger and lice,
they bothered me terribly. I lay in a large room
where the Russian soldiers were dying far from
home. In the morning I would notice the empty

beds. I was the only boy in that ward and they called me "Pacan (pronounced Patzan—a teenager in Russian)." I got used to the name, and responded to it, which usually got me a piece of bread from a dying soldier.

From Wilno I got to a place called Laski. There I grazed cows again. I slept in a tiny corner of my fathers' supposed friend's place and I recognized the rug that hung over my bed before the war.

*On September 1, 1946 Zborowiecki brought me to the Jewish Committee. They placed me in Helenowek where I went to school for the first time. From that time I remember a particularly nasty kid by the name of Henry Grynberg (*he became a writer of some renown). *I heard later that he became the chairman of the school Youth Organization (ZMP) and acted in a play by Kruczkowski.*[1]

The year 1947 was remarkable because of the brothers Cyngiser. When Bronek said that he did

---

[1]   Leon Kruczkowski, a Polish playwright revered by the communist establishment because of his strongly leftist sympathies long before it became profitable

*not want to be a Jew, I agreed. It was a feeling
shared by many of us.*[2]

*In Helenowek I took part in many activities,
building a storage cellar, working in a joiner's shop
and on Sundays I was responsible for the children
who took up the duties of the adult personnel for the
day. On Saturdays, I labored for many hours to
compile a fair and just list of duties for the children
for Sunday.*

*Helenowek imbued us with high ethical standards
that do not exist anymore in this world. I do not
think this was good. Having traveled around the
world since 1962, I found humanity at the lowest
ethical levels in history. The honesty instilled by
Helenowek did not help. In Helenowek I was not
hungry, but I longed for the place where my home
was. It was called Ponaryszki, I missed the forests,
the meadows and the river. I was happy there.*

---

[2] To think of it, I myself never had that feeling. I remember hatred and
defiance and no way would I want to be of any of the species that came
after me and destroyed my family, be it German, Pole or whoever. But
many children of that time although knowing that they were Jews
wished they weren't.

Akiwa is not untypical of the traumatized kids who later became doctors, engineers and craftsmen. I saw him off when he was leaving Poland for Israel in 1957. He came

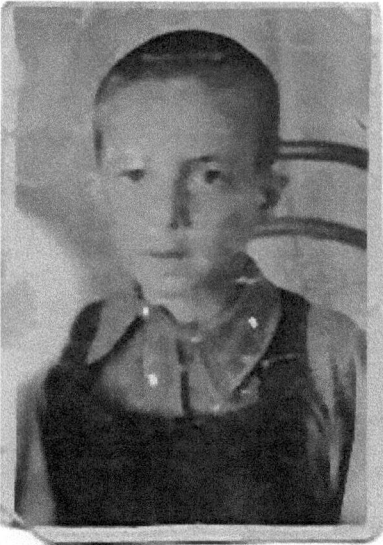

to Warsaw from a coal mine in Silesia where he worked as a technician. He was run down and again had the appearance of a hunted animal. He had a sharp knife in his pocket for self-defense. Akiwa had been restless throughout his life. His spirit seems no to have had a moment of tranquility. He now lives, financially secure in Israel, but in an ever-present mental turmoil. The past haunting him like it does every one of us.

Akiwa died in February 2013 at the age of 77 in Israel

These were the types of cases Mrs. Falkowska had to deal with.

Slowly the community of children stabilized, and if there were new arrivals they were not so dramatic anymore, because the horrible finds came to an end and new children placed in the orphanage had some relatives bringing them in.

Milstein had perfect material to mold; bewildered kids, under her control for 24 hours and indoctrinated in school, not unlike the Janissaries[3] trained by the Moslems. The first order of business for her was to see if she could organize a Party cell among the orphanage's adult personnel. This was always the first duty and priority of a comrade. That was somewhat difficult because no one was inclined to join and the subjects were not that suitable. All the people concerned were Holocaust survivors and exhausted. Politics were the furthest thing from their minds. The exception was Mr. Bryl, a guard. The remarkable thing

---

[3] Janissaries [Turkish, - recruits], elite corps in the service of the Ottoman Empire (Turkey). It was composed of war captives and Christian youths pressed into service; all the recruits were converted to Islam and trained under the strictest discipline.

about Mr. Bryl was that he was a veteran of the Spanish Civil War who got his jaw broken by a rifle butt blow to his face from a fascist soldier. He sometimes walked around with his gun strapped to his side. We kept extracting from Mr. Bryl glorious stories from the war where he put his jaw on the line in the shining cause of happiness for mankind. Comrade Milstein was skeptical about Bryl and not happy about our adulation for him. Why? He hadn't made up his life story, it was all in his dossier and Milstein did not deny it when we asked. Mr. Bryl kept his distance from Milstein too. I could guess why, much, much later, when I learned a little about communist actions in that bloody Spanish fiasco for the reds. They were as busy murdering each other as fighting the so-called fascists [1]. Mr. Bryl ended up in Israel, became a farmer and lived out his life there. Finally having achieved a degree of spiritual tranquility he died in 1996. For a while then, Milstein was alone, and, as the rules required, she had to be a member of a cell elsewhere and report there, so we had an unofficial commissar amongst us. We, our principal and everyone else as well had to be careful, because one word from Milstein could spell trouble for anyone. Being a naïve kid at the time it is difficult for me to say now, what went on behind the scenes. I can only say that the personnel were stable, no one disappeared in the middle of the night or was hauled away by the KGB (the Polish equivalent was the UB—the Bureau for Internal Security). She was given a free hand in indoctrination, but the other Mentors pursued their own way of teaching and dealing with the kids.

The political and social conditions in Poland favored indoctrination or brainwashing, if one prefers that term. There were, however, some spoilers.

The Favorable Conditions

We, the children, were all in shock after our war years' experience, totally confused as to what to think of the world around us. How could all that have happened? I myself sought some explanation or at least most some assurances that this was a horrible aberration in human history, never to be repeated. The explanation given by Milstein was simple, " It is all the fault of capitalism, it is rotting and in its end stage it produces fascism. What we have experienced, is the last paroxysm of that rotten system. The new shining path for mankind, communism, will not allow such a calamity to ever occur again." Of course at that time I was far from ready to point out that communism had already committed atrocities comparable to or exceeding those of fascism. That realization would come to me in the future. At that time the only thing we knew was that the Red Army had defeated the forces of darkness and had saved our lives. There was a Russian army unit stationed nearby, as was the case throughout Poland at the time. One of their tasks was to guard the orphanage from possible attack by Polish "reactionary and anti-Semitic rioters or the armed anticommunist underground".

The threat was real and we were very concerned and frightened. It was the time of Kielce, a town where a few barely alive Jewish holocaust survivors were nursing themselves back to life. A Polish mob, incited by officials, as was eventually disclosed, after the fall of communism [2] killed 47 weak and defenseless Jews in a pogrom on July 14, 1946. We were frightened and armed ourselves illegally. The orphanage personnel turned a blind eye to it. Most of our weapons came from those Russian troops. We got them by begging and trading small items, but mostly by pestering the officers until they gave us surplus stuff. Eventually we acquired impressive firepower including submachine guns. Once again to us, the Russians were the good guys, and we dismissed their misbehavior in the neighborhood, where some of the soldiers were stealing from the farmers or committing other misdeeds. These incidents troubled us, and we ran to comrade Milstein for explanations, which she always had. We forgot about the occurrences that did not so neatly fit into Milstein's glorification of the Soviet Union soon after these troops moved out. We wondered later how it was possible for those who experienced Soviet life (Milstein survived the war in the Soviet Union) not to become disillusioned and to continue to peddle that ideology, which should be considered by any standards as willful and criminal misrepresentation of reality. She was not alone, there were a slew of such believers who came with the Red Army and were the instruments of Stalin's scheme to communize Polish society, which was historically anti-Soviet. A lot of those, were idealistic Jews who held the misguided belief that they would build a better brand of communism, their own. This is still the mantra of the contemporary left, here in the US and in Europe, in academia and elsewhere—"We will do it better." Those stupid, well-meaning bastards, they don't know what they are talking about. For us, at that time, the overriding concerns were elsewhere. We were in danger and under anti-Semitic harassment at school; we also had to learn furiously to make up the lost years. Milstein characterized Anti-Semitism and the Kielce massacre as the last vestiges of a rotten system, one that the communists were struggling to eradicate from the face of the earth. There is no question that she naively and with her whole heart believed in what she was teaching or rather preaching. She later paid with her life for that exorbitantly fervent belief.

The Spoilers

Initially most of the kids from the orphanage went to school in the nearby suburb of Radogoszcz. In the early days when communism had not been yet consolidated and had not managed to put every facet of public or private life under its control, the schools continued their traditional prewar way of teaching. We had the old textbooks and the prewar teachers, who basically were anticommunists; we therefore had to deal with a lot of contradictions between school and comrade Milstein. We also had Ms. Lucy Gold directly responsible for our "middle-aged" group. She was a prewar Mentor and a survivor of Auschwitz, had no idea of what communism was all about and did not care. In the evenings when we were all in bed she read to us romantic stories from the American Civil War. She liked America and obviously we had a mass of questions; the answers were in sharp contrast with comrade Milstein's teachings. All this and the school-sown seeds soon went dormant for a good while after communism silenced any politically-incorrect ideas or expressions. Nevertheless this early exposure to knowledge later forbidden in school and life sank in deep and burst to the surface in some of us at the time we entered university and professional life. Interestingly, not all of us had experienced these awakenings from the deep ingrained deception. And, more interestingly, that "awakening" occurred, though not exclusively, in those who came from the middle or upper class especially the bourgeois from which I came. The kids in school who had a strong family tradition of anti-sovietism were much less vulnerable to indoctrination, they went into a deep hiding mode where they perfunctorily went along with the trappings of socialism just to wait it out. A good illustration of that was what happened after Stalin's death in 1953. The feeling of loss was very profound for some part of the population; it was a feeling akin to facing a catastrophe—what will humanity do now, without the guidance of that wise father of nations. Those who were in the waiting mode rejoiced or had a lot of fun with the somber official mourning. My future wife Elizabeth remembered wetting her panties one time from jokes and laughter as she and her teen-age friends engaged in brazen mocking at one of many official events of mourning, and wailing where attendance was compulsory.

This elementary school exemplified Polish society's attitude toward the pitiful remnants of the Jewish holocaust survivors and, worse, to the children. It dramatically lessened the influence it could have had in immunizing us against the indoctrination of likes of comrade Milstein and especially those that came later, when the indoctrination pressure became intense in the special schools we were sent to. There were two aspects to that anti-Semitic harassment. The Polish kids were constantly casting slurs and the boys would pick fights with us. The teachers reinforced that atmosphere. Religion was an important part of the school's curriculum and some of the teachers would use it as a tool to humiliate us. Lectures always began with a Catholic prayer at the beginning of the school day and the instruction to us was:

"All Jews should stand at attention when Christian children pray."

We, the Jewish kids, had to leave the classroom and wait out the hours of religious instruction in the hallways. We knew that the kids were whipped onto pity for Christ's lot, which was blamed on the Jews. The Polish kids tore into us every so often after these priest instructors left the school premises. I can remember their pious faces with the sinister smile of holy mischief well done. That school became a torturous path of learning.

One day the history teacher said:

"Sven, I would like you to stay a while after school, I need to talk to you."

I waited to be told the following, and I remember it verbatim more than fifty years later.

"Sven, I want you to know that you are excellent in history, but I can not give you an "A," because I would be accused by other teachers of unduly favoring Jews. I wanted you to know, so as not to discourage you from studying. That is all."

This incredible intolerance of us in the face of what had happened was and is amazing. The Poles were aware of the brutal annihilation of the Jewish population, they were witnesses to it and they themselves were subject to much of that German brutality, yet they did not have the humanity to at least leave us alone. That pushed us further into the realm of comrade Milstein's world, at least to think that maybe her vision as it pertained to the Jewish question might have some validity. Little did we know, at that time, about the communist movement's history of perverse and complex anti-Semitism and especially Stalin's actions and attitudes. So we slogged through our days in Poland and witnessed a steady tightening of control over public life. We were later sent to special schools that were free of religious instruction. These schools were called TPD (The Friends of Children Society) and were state run like the others but were under the Communist Party ideological control. They were designated as model schools that would make inroads into the whole system, to eliminate all religion and to remake all the schools in their mold. This was eventually was accomplished nationwide.

In the meantime life in the orphanage ran smoothly, sheltered from the outside world once we got home from school, which was virtually our only outside contact. Essentially life was good—we learned, worked and played and had a sense of purpose and progress. The ideological pressure came from comrade Milstein; the other personnel could not have cared less about any specific ideology and went on with what is considered normal life. Milstein's emphasis was on rooting out religion first. Religion is an obvious competitor for the control of minds and souls. Communism adopted the first commandment and applied it to itself. ***"I am the Lord thy God.... Thou shalt have no other gods before me."*** She succeeded splendidly. It was easy; the fundamental question to ask was " How could God allow such a calamity to take place if he existed or was ever in control?" We all came from religious homes, my parents were religious and my father took me to the synagogue every Saturday; they never lost faith even in the face of the greatest adversity. Comrade Milstein however washed our faith away so thoroughly that it never returned. An interesting occurrence took place in the orphanage some time later after the war. New Jewish kids became scarce, and the available spaces were allocated to Polish children. At one time we got a load of them from a Catholic convent, in line with curtailing religious upbringing. Catholic nuns in institutions attached to a convent had raised these teenage kids. Without exception each of them could not have been more cynical about religion. That was a surprise to us, and of course it was water for comrade Milstein's mill. I knew exactly what the source of that cynicism was from Cynthia, one of the girls, whom I describe in my memoirs under the title "Very Intimately Personal."

The trauma of the war years slowly subsided and the indoctrination effort was more subtle, not too burdensome, and moreover we concerned ourselves with teenager's stuff. Whatever time was left after school and home chores, was devoted to sports, reading, pranks on girls. A good part of the time was devoted to inducing the personnel to tell us stories from their lives. There were a number of these people, kitchen staff, guards, and workers on the premises of our rather large establishment, not forgetting our school truck driver. The most colorful guys were the guards recruited among demobilized, Soviet and Polish soldiers.

I will dwell here for a moment on some of the personalities who etched themselves into our memories. Of course as adolescents, having grown up mostly without a normal family setting and feeling our hormones, become active, we became very interested in the lives of the adults around us, and always provoked some discussion on taboo subjects which we could not discuss with our Mentors. The adults were all very caring and helpful. Here are some memory bits about those people who attempted to live their lives without interference from the comrades and who kept a good distance from Milstein.

Mr. Godlewski

Godlewski came to us from a mental institution. He marched into Poland with the Polish army and went to his home village trying to find his family. On arriving he learned that his entire family had been hidden and sheltered from being taken to an extermination camp by a local Polish farmer. As was often the case some scum betrayed the set-up to the Germans and Godlewski's family perished together with the Polish farmer's. Godlewski took his submachine gun and killed the entire family of the informer. He went into such an uncontrollable mental state that he was declared insane, discharged from the army and placed in one of the infamous mental institutions near Warsaw, called Tworki. Upon release he was placed with us as a guard. I vividly remember him from an incident in the forest where we went to try out my submachine gun assembled from parts obtained from a Russian officer. I was concerned about getting into trouble for that and worried that somebody might hear the shooting, spot us and inform the authorities. Mr. Godlewski's answer was:

" Do not worry one little bit, I have my papers from
the crazies house, they can do nothing to us."
Godlewskis's tales of his wartime exploits were
inexhaustible. We liked to listen to how he always came
out on top of any situation with the Germans. At times his
behavior was a bit strange, but we liked Mr. Godlewski.

The Lifschitz Family.

Marisa was short and had some kind of physical
impairment. She walked with a limp, slightly bent over.
She was the Mentor of the very young kids, so we were not
often in contact with her. She seemed to be a nice person.
Her husband Moses was a guard and they lived in one of
the utility buildings. Squabbles broke out between them
and they usually became public. One I could not forget,
because it seemed so exciting and bizarre at the time. I
heard Marisa shouting loudly at Mr. Lifschitz. I went closer
and asked her what was the matter, why was she so angry,
Mr. Lifschitz seemed to be such a nice guy. Her response in
a raised voice was:

"I told him so many times, when he ejaculates, he
should do it into a bucket. So much stuff is coming
out that I have to wash the linen every time and how

many times a week can I do it in my condition?! He

could fill a bucket full in no time!

Mr. Lifcshitz would smile gently and say nothing.

Otherwise they were a very loving couple.

Mr. Korn

I only remember Mr. Korn because of his
extremely fat wife (she was our seamstress) and a short
incident on the stairs of the main house. We always pitied
him and wondered how he did it with Bella. We challenged
each other to finally ask him about that, but none of the
youngsters had the courage or audacity to do it. One time I
talked to Mr. Korn standing on the stairs of the main house.
I was contemplating delicately settling the matter for my
friends without offending the so very nice Mr. Korn.
Suddenly a girl, the daughter of one of the greenhouse
workers, strolled by. She was about seventeen and very
shapely, a poster girl for Nazi propaganda art for Arian
beauty, blond, tall and lovely. Mr. Korn fixed his gaze on
her exquisitely formed behind and, licking his lips, said:

"You know, that girl is ripe for plucking,

somebody should consider going after her."

The expression on his face was one of sadness and
resignation.

Ms. Martha and Mr. Mitelstadt

    Ms. Martha was a German woman who did not flee westward with the retreating German army. There were a number of them working the greenhouse. They were essentially free, but under restriction not to travel and loosely watched. Ms. Martha was the chief in the kitchen, and the kitchen was a place of high interest to all of us. Not that we were starving, but we had structured meals and allocations. The economic situation in Poland after the war was not very good. With our high physical activity we were always on the look-out for a snack. This is where Ms. Martha came in; she always set aside some basics to give us when we came by to say hello. She was a beautiful woman in her thirties and the epitome of kindness and caring; we liked her very much. Soon we noticed Mr. Mitelstadt, a gray-haired, tall, stooped man, who was one of the handymen, a Mr. fix-it who hung around Martha quite a lot. Eventually they got married and later emigrated to Germany under the German repatriation action. What an ironic twist of events, a Jew, a holocaust survivor, marrying a German. That perhaps was understandable in the case of Ms. Martha, we all loved her, but moving to Germany?! I guess any means of escape from communism was acceptable. Some people had an instinctive foreboding of things to come. On our first visit to New York after coming to the U.S. we met the owner of the motel where we stayed; he was from Poland.

"I escaped in 1945, right after the war ended."

"You did the right thing obviously, what exactly prompted you to be so smart?"

"My uncle in America was sending packages with coffee. I used to sell the coffee (a sought-after commodity) and bought necessities. One day I was summoned to the KGB (UB) and interrogated about who was sending the packages, why so much coffee and what was I doing with it?"

"Yeah, it figures."

"Right after that I decided to run. I had no idea about anything political, but I figured that if they could interrogate me about a pound of coffee, I had better put the greatest distance possible between these guys and my persona."

Contrary to our approach to Ms. Martha we avoided any contact with the other Germans working in the greenhouse. We saw them going about their jobs in sullen moods, like automatons. We often wondered if they did fully realize what their nation had done? What did they think and feel. Were they regretful, did they suffer pangs of conscience? They could see with their own eyes the crippled, barely alive remnants of their nation's handiwork. Well, I got an answer to that. I was returning with mother from town. There was a long walk from the suburban tram station to our compound. The last stretch leading to the premises was a beautiful tree-lined alley. A few yards behind us was a group of those greenhouse Germans going to work. At some point, when we were not far from the house, they started mocking my mother, making sarcastic remarks about her being German and marrying and siding with the Jews. I have many regrets about my behavior in the past; mostly for timidity, and this incident makes me furious at myself even today, fifty-five years later. I should have grabbed a few stones and stoned those bastards; I was very proficient in stone throwing. My Mother did not respond, we walked in silence, and she never commented on it, dismissing it like she did a lot of the evil she suffered from people. It gives me great sorrow to think that only now do I understand the suffering our mother went through merely for one decision in her life, marrying my father, a Jew. Regrets of past omissions are very common, in my case so much more painful because of the immensity of what she went through for us. It must be noted and it gives credit to the Jewish communities along our life journey, whether in the ghettos or in the time after the war in the orphanage where she worked in the kitchen, that she was fully accepted without any problems. When she got ill she had the best treatment available at the time and was placed in an up-scale sanatorium. There was no limit to her sacrifice for us, her children. After the war there was a drive for overseas adoptions out of the orphanage, and a couple from Australia wanted to adopt my sister and me. Our mother wanted to go along with that, for our sake. I was somewhat proud, when recalling this incident in later years. I flatly refused and did not even want to discuss it, although there were all kinds of good reasons for it being put forward by the people around us and by our mother herself. When that issue was over, I could see that my behavior gave my mother some comfort.

Jerry Fraszczyk

Our driver was another memorable character. He drove us to school in the morning and collected some of us in the afternoon; some came home by themselves from closer schools. A modern school bus it was not; we were packed like sardines in the cargo hold of a large Bedford truck obtained from the American military lend-lease supplies. Through the years there was not a single mishap, a lot of fun though, teasing girls.

Fraszczyk was a tall skinny guy with a fair and densely freckled complexion. He had a large bony face with a mane of red hair. He came to us from the army, where he had been a Soviet tank crewman. We pestered him for tales of his wartime exploits and especially his successes with women. His tales about that were so graphic that they became a splendid substitute for pornographic material, which of course was unthinkable for us to obtain or ever to look at. We also admired him for his mechanical skills in keeping the old Bedford running. I was always around him whenever he was fixing something. We also admired his colorful dress and especially the nice half boots he said he stripped from a dead German officer. One day I saw a silhouette in the distance moving toward the compound that looked somewhat familiar. Coming closer I recognized Mr. Fraszczyk with a large bundle under his arm, but barefoot.

"Mr. Fraszczyk, what happened to your boots?"

"I sold them and bought a bunch of books, I am going to college."

I met Fraszczyk later on in college. He was ahead of me by a year or two and in constant trouble for his manner of dressing. It was dangerous to wear striped socks that resembled the kind that were fashionable in the west. Fraszczyk finished college with some difficulty, worked a little bit as an engineer and emigrated to Israel in the second post-war wave of Jews leaving Poland, in 1957. This was the second opportunity to leave communism after the initial opportunity in 1945 ended in total closure, it came, as result of internal upheaval in the Soviet block and in Poland in particular (more on this later). I heard later that he committed suicide in Israel. This is how colorful lives slide into oblivion, and there is no one willing and talented enough to pass on the life story of a Fraszczyk to future generations.

Nurse Kaplan

Nurse Kaplan was in charge of our health. She was physically a robust woman, pleasant, not very attractive but not ugly either. She was a mixture of terror and amiability. Terror when she performed her duties. It was very difficult to keep our large community of kids out of health related dangers. Any infection would spread like wildfire among kids living and sleeping in close quarters. Her goal was to keep the isolation ward empty and she accomplished that with ruthless efficiency. Terrors included her periodic head inspections and keeping haircuts very short at all times. Then there were the humiliating genital inspections in the shower room where we had to stand in line and Nurse Kaplan, still a young woman,

Nurse Kaplan

would go from boy to boy (I was fourteen) and thoroughly inspect everybody's penis and vicinity (We called it schwanz (tail) parade). This was often the site of parasitic infections brought back from school. An infected kid would be ashamed to disclose it, and before long it would spread despite the strictly enforced draconian hygiene of Nurse Kaplan. In spite of that we liked Nurse Kaplan, for when she was not on her designated mission and on duty she would tell us stories and dirty jokes. She also helped us with our Russian language homework. Her approach to everyday life issues was straightforward; she did not beat around the bush. Crude and simple; we liked that very much as a refreshing change from the lofty approaches in school and from the officially approved manner of behavior. On her days off she went to the city on Saturdays to see her boyfriend. She would sometimes say:

> "I am going for some love games with my boyfriend in town. Behave while am out, see you on Monday."

We tried to get a little revenge for the Schwanz (tail) parades in the shower room by scratching off a bit of the paint on the outside shower room window. We waited to catch a glimpse her taking a shower. We managed

eventually to get an opportunity; I was at the hole having a good look into the shower room when suddenly she looked up as if spotting something and guessed what was going on. She bent over to
show her rather robust behind to the window. That was the end of our peeping on Nurse Kaplan.

Nurse Kaplan eventually went to Israel and died there an old, lonely and abandoned woman. She died in a shabby nursing home, booted out of her home by the children of her last, late husband. Some of the orphanage children who ended up in Israel occasionally kept in touch with her, but that proved difficult in later years because she stopped recognizing people. There were numerous other people who entered our lives, but they were less colorful and our memories are less vivid. They were all exceptionally decent. Some went so far as to help some of the kids who went to college by sending money from their meager salaries. A good example of this was generosity was Mr. Holland, the accountant.

One other factor was added to this caldron of nationalities, politics and the goings-on in our everyday lives. This was the Zionist movement, whose advocates came to lobby us children to emigrate to Palestine. Since communism was not yet in total control they could do it. Their rationale seemed to be irrefutable; they argued, *"We were not wanted here anyway, how could we live in a cemetery where our people's remains were scattered so that we did not even know where their graves were? This Polish nation had such an awful record of persecution and aiding the Germans against us, it will never get rid of that mean spirit. We need to build Jewish nationhood to finally end this eternal string of calamities befalling us with regularity through the ages."* We were torn apart, ping-pong balls between comrade Milstein and the Zionist agitators. Milstein promised the eradication of anti-Semitism, a shining future of brotherhood and social justice. The agonizing about this was excruciating. A lot of children decided to go with the Zionists. Those who were too tired or did not dare to plunge into the unknown after all they had suffered, stayed. Eventually after years most ended up in Israel anyway, but that was yet to come. My mother tried to take advantage of the possibility to leave Poland and took us out of the orphanage into a kibbutz that had formed in the city in preparation for leaving for Palestine. Her strategy was to first get us out of Poland; she had had enough of Poland. Besides, that was about the only way to escape from communism during those early years, and she instinctively hated communism, although without much understanding. Our Zionist careers ended quickly. My mother got ill and ended up in a sanatorium and we children were back in the orphanage under the mentorship of comrade Milstein, our journey back into commie-land began in earnest. Mother died in 1949 of tuberculosis and heart failure in the hospital. She is buried in the Jewish cemetery in Lodz.

I was not the best material for comrade Milstein to work with. Shy in first encounters with people, an introvert and rather distrustful. I was adamantly against joining any youth organization. The Party drove hard to put youth into established, controllable organizations whose trappings were supposed to attract. The Hitlerjugend is a prime example, so are the Soviet Pioneers. In Polish society there was the strong, long-standing tradition of a Boy Scout movement. It was non-political, and if anything its teachings were at odds with communist ideology. The Party tried frantically to get that under control. They tried to form competing organizations under their control for each age group. Eventually they only succeeded in forming one for the older youth, the ZMP (Alliance Of Polish Youth) and laboriously managed to get control over the Boy Scouts.

The orphanage formed the Young Pioneers a counterweight to the Scouts; it was not enough to have the kids under constant control after all. In the familiar surroundings of the orphanage I was not as shy among my peers and soon showed some leadership capabilities, which lead to my being appointed to organizational functions concerned with our daily lives and the children's council. However I would not join a structure with fanfare to facilitate political teachings. Because of my status the pressure on me mounted, but I would not yield. This was not because of any political awareness, but I felt that all those drills and marches, uniforms and saluting were ridiculous and beneath my serious consideration.

"Domestic" Pioneers being instructed by
Bronek Cyngiser.

**I can only guess the subject; I stubbornly stayed away.
It was 1949**

Sitting second from the right is Akiwa Brand, fifth is Jerry
Frydman. Standing before the last on the left is Jerry
Dulman, and the last one sitting is Daniel Witelski, in the
USA since 1968; his life story would be great material for a
literary giant like John Steinbeck. Daniel is living a
torturous, bizarre and horrifying life, so much so that one
wonders if there is anyone watching from above. The only
decent times Daniel has had, it seems, were the orphanage
and school years. He was an A student, but that did not help

him any when he entered adulthood. We have lost track of
a few of those in the picture, but we know where most of
them are and what they are doing.

The Pioneers within the orphanage did not last long.
There simply was no time left for this obvious silliness
after homework and chores, the important stuff had been
done. Nevertheless "they" tried to put this layer of control
over the already existing ones, even though every minute of
our time throughout the day had been already filled and
organized. There was no need for these "pioneers." After
school we ate a meal, a short recess followed and then
homework was done and checked by the Tutor and only
after that, was there time for games, reading or activity
such as woodworking or whatever the kids liked to do. This
time was precious, but sometimes it was interrupted
because small domestic chores had to be done. On days
when school was out we had to do larger domestic tasks.
Somebody tried to cut short the time we had to ourselves
for what everybody regarded as silliness, but it did not
work. The kids just did not go along. In the photo one can
see obvious skepticism and boredom on some of the faces,
even though that photograph was probably staged. I do not
remember whose idea it was, but it goes to the credit of

Mrs. Falkowska that she could see the futility of it and let it die rather quickly. She certainly had to give it a try since the idea probably came from Milstein.

The reader might wonder why girls have not been mentioned so far. There was about an equal number of girls in the orphanage of all ages up to just before college age, which was about eighteen. Nowadays such a situation would be fraught with all kinds of trouble and difficulties for the teachers and perhaps considered "explosive." That yet was not the case at all; we were treated equally with a de-emphasis of gender differences in learning duties and games. There was no obstacle for a girl if she wanted to join a volleyball team. We had a song and dance group under the direction of a renowned choreographer and the girls gravitated there along some boys. Of course we had romances here and there, all platonic and well-tolerated, **no pregnancies**. Sex was taboo reserved for later and for marriage. Inter-gender relationship could not have been smoother. Though, practical jokes were quite frequent. The biggest pranksters were Jacob and his buddy Richard. To give just a sample of their ingenuity, I need to recall the following incident. They sneaked unseen into the older girls' bedroom and poured some water under haughty

Julia's bed. Then they ran around collecting spectators to see how Julia had wetted her bed at night. They collected a huge crowd; everybody wanted to see Julia's mishap with their own eyes. Jacob and Richard then had to apologize publicly to Julia at a specially called meeting, their happiness about the whole affair quite obviously showing on their faces while they apologized as directed.

Since all our Tutors were women, the girls were able to get the basics and emotional support during their transition times to womanhood. The boys as mentioned, got some of that from the adult male personnel, not always in the proper form. Nurse Kaplan, was very helpful to both— the girls and the boys. Some married after leaving the orphanage; I was one of the few who did. Many of us men keep in touch with "the girls" to this day; they are all scattered around the world, from St. Louis where Felicia Wertz lives to Denmark where Erna, one of our more vivacious "sisters" lives. Unfortunately I have few photographs. This co-ed environment requires a separate story. I have not attempted to tell it here to avoid straying from my basic theme of describing the political and social environment in which I lived in Poland under communism.

FELICIA 1966

I did well in school; the only disastrous areas were composition, grammar and spelling, quite enough to keep me from passing the all important maturity test, which was a passage to college. I did very well in most of the other subjects, especially math and physics. Because of those marks the teachers' body showed some leniency. A now funny and memorable incident occurred at the time our group was nearing the end of high school and it was time to decide what guidance should be given to individual kids about their direction in life. Our director Mrs. Falkowska had a young psychiatrist friend and she thought it an excellent idea to test the kids for various aptitudes. She was a young lady with a slender, shapely figure, shining thick chestnut hair arranged in a chignon with lighter streaks almost blond on her left side; a lady out of my adolescent dreams. The psychiatrist, Ms. Maleviak gave me all her tests. After it was over Mrs. Falkowska called me in and said,

"Sven, you did very poorly on the test. Ms. Malewiak said that you appear to be of very sluggish apprehension and she thinks your intelligence level is only fit for you to become a carpenter at best. Did you do this on purpose?"

"Absolutely not, director, I tried to do my best. I must say that she is a very beautiful woman and her hair is just the way I always dreamed it would be, if I ever got a girlfriend."

I badly wanted to become an aircraft design engineer, which was considered one of the toughest branches of the engineering school, with very limited admittance and high entry barriers! I carried that assessment of my abilities into college and into my professional life, never able to forget that incident. Ms. Maleviak's predictive powers did not match her beauty in another case as well. There was this tall boy who had lost his arm during the war, Jerry Frydman. The remarkable thing about him was that he would not accept any special favors because of his condition. In the morning, when we had limited time to make our beds, dress and lace up our shoes—just like boot camp—he achieved such perfection with his one arm that he was always ready before most of the other kids. Ms. Maleviak rated him as fit only to become a brush maker. Jerry ended up being a successful professor of mathematics in Lodz and later in Israel.

In retrospect, I see that I was blessed with a firm and unswerving desire to get an education in engineering. The only other strong passion permeating me was girls, which proved to be an incapacitating factor. Fortunately I was not like some of the other kids, who were clueless about what they wanted to do and ended up being lifelong Communist Party functionaries, courtesy of comrade Milstein's indoctrination. Some others went into the humanities, and that required active participation in political activities, a display of loyalty to Party goals and some zeal. A number went to medical school and this will bring me to the communist brand of affirmative action, but first a few words about the TPD schools. I shied away from involvement in political action as much as I could, mainly because of my other interests and mistrust of anything political. Nevertheless I was curious about attaining some sort of world view, some sort of guiding life philosophy. Generally, apart from comrade Milstein's pushing of the Marxist interpretation of the world we also had the "old fashioned "Ten Commandments with some modifications. The biggest modification was the tenet that Party pronouncements took precedent over anything else, and these might change from day to day, no matter what was moral yesterday. We were told that the principles of *some* of the Ten Commandments were self-evident social principles and that God was superfluous. At that stage, I was listening, reading and searching without being firmly convinced of any Marxist theory, but it slowly started rubbing in at the edges. The example given to us to emulate was that of a Soviet boy, Pavlik Morozov, [3] "a hero" who overheard his parents making anti-Soviet remarks and denounced them to the authorities. They were arrested and sent to the gulag, and Pavlik continued his loyal and happy life without them in a state orphanage (we were not told that he did not live long or what precisely happened to him). That seemed to us a crazy set of motivations or events; we still remembered our parents and the bond between us. We were, after all, defiant holocaust survivors and this and similar crap never soiled my conscience or that of any of the kids in the orphanage. We survived by chance, but often more so because we were instinctively able to correctly and to our benefit evaluate information coming our way.

TPD No. 1

The TPD schools were established to make inroads into the educational system in order to rid it of religious instruction. Since the Polish nation was Catholic and the church had its traditional firm grip on spiritual and social life in Poland, it was not advisable to change that situation by decree. The Party decided to take it slowly but relentlessly and to curtail the power of the church on many fronts. Anti-religious agitation and propaganda became furious and chicanery against the church was practiced wherever possible. We were relieved when we landed in the TPDs, because finally we no longer had to deal with expression of anti-Semitism; it was absolutely forbidden, and we breathed freely. No more humiliating remarks from teachers, no more fights and slurs. The school population was composed of children of Party members or of children from suitably progressive social backgrounds, with a good sprinkling of children of Jewish origin. All Jewish parents were eager to get their children into these schools for the above-mentioned reasons. In my age group therefore there were a number of Jewish children who were from non-communist, Zionist, backgrounds. These were quickly declared enemies of the people and though tolerated, became "second class citizens" and had to step gingerly, with their heads down, not giving anyone an excuse to expel them or take political action against them. Most of them were marking time in Poland, waiting for an opportunity to escape. It was easy enough for the adult political "organizers," who were present in every such school, to create a charged political atmosphere and set one group of kids against the other. Even though this school had much higher standards and better teachers, it nevertheless became a preview of later conditions under communism, where honesty, integrity, uprightness and loyalty became empty terms.

There was, in our class, a nice plump Jewish girl by the name of Zielinska (a polonized name from the Jewish Greenberg; she turned out not to be so green). She "fell in love" with a fellow named Ziental. Ziental was of working class background, a factory worker's son, very low on the prewar social scale, which could not be more perfect. Zielinska however was a petty bourgeoisie; her parents owned a very small shop of some kind—that was still allowed. It was very fashionable to attach oneself to pure working class circles, at least mingle with them. These class distinctions were very important. Worker or peasant background (the poorer the better) were tickets to all kinds of promotions and advantages. Zielinska brought Ziental very nice lunch sandwiches every day, which he accepted for a while. Then after some time Ziental had a change of heart and asked Zielinska not to bring him sandwiches any more, but the girl would not stop and insisted that he accept them— true love and concern for an "undernourished" worker's son. Later came the weekly meeting of our youth organization, ZMP (Alliance of Polish Youth), an extension of the Communist Party. At that time I was one of the rare holdouts and not yet a member, but dutifully attended the weekly meeting since they purportedly dealt with general classroom concerns.

The Chairman:

"Any other issues today?"

Ziental:

"Comrade Chairman, I have a problem. Zielinska is pursuing me and stubbornly bringing me lunches, which I refuse. I do not want any favors from somebody who has bourgeois views and with whom I do not agree ideologically. I am hereby asking her, in the presence of all my colleagues, to desist, and if she does not I am asking our organization to take steps against her."

The Chairman:

> "I hereby ask colleague Zielinska to stop bringing lunches for Ziental. This will be noted in the proceedings of this meeting."

Next meeting, again, "Any issues left?"

Zielinska:

> Comrade Chairman, I would like our organization to check information I have obtained, regarding colleague Ziental's father who was a member of the reactionary Union of Support for the fascist government in prewar Poland and therefore is not fit to be in our organization."

The Chairman:

> "It is so noted, we will check the information."

The information was confirmed and Ziental lost his mantle of origin purity and any possibility of favored treatment, for college admission, for example.

We all were hardly children anymore; around sixteen, give or take a year or two. This sequence of events etched itself into my memory for its shocking implications. It basically meant that private matters had been politicized, and a government organization had "to solve" these issue. What shocked me most was the eagerness with which the members meddled in private lives, and their ruthlessness and totally unprincipled behavior in using any foul means to achieve an objective. I did not verbalize all this at the time, but felt, "There was something rotten in the kingdom of Denmark."

Of course we the orphanage children were pretty much isolated from the goings on of society at large. We were not aware of the arrests, the disappearances, intimidation of workers, and the ruthless campaign against the remnants of the private sector: the small shopkeepers, artisans and vegetable growers around the city. As I have stated Zielinska's family ran a small shop of some kind.

By now, we were close to finishing high school and anxiety arose about getting into college. One of my good friends, Ed Butermilk who had the purest of social origins, who excelled in sports and was universally liked, got elected General Chairman of our school Youth Organization. He took me aside one day and said,

> "Sven, my friend, you are among the very few who have not joined. The organization does not care about most of the trashy leftovers; they are outcasts. But I cannot understand why you are holding out, it

is sheer stupidity, you will not get into college that way."

That did it; I joined, about a year before finishing high school. I tried to show a little bit of politically positive activity to become a member in good standing. Ed in the meantime became hugely popular. This went on for a short while until a very important meeting was announced. Three regional Party Committee members came to the meeting, one of them presiding.

"Comrades, we your elder brothers in the Party, have become concerned about the very dangerous situation in your school. The Napoleonic tendencies of your chairman Ed Buttermilk have corrupted the upper management of your organization. He ignores the instructions coming from us, does not conduct the proper political activities and rules like dictator. The full list of specific charges will be read now by comrade such and such."

This was done, and after a short discussion a vote was taken to remove Ed from his office; the voting was by raising hands. The conference room was packed.

"Who is in favor of the motion to remove Ed Buttermilk from office?"

It seemed that everybody was.

"Who is against?"

Mine was the only hand raised. The shock and subsequent fear for my college chances were great, but I never did regret that vote, ever.

It was announced that the Government had a program to send a number of college candidates to the Soviet Union to be educated in the best and most progressive universities in the world. Applications would be taken within the school; I applied. An added benefit was a scholarship triple the one that could be expected domestically, and I was destitute, not a penny to my soul. After a while I was called into the principal's office, to see director Czerwinski, a very nice fellow.

> "Sven, I have a sad mission to perform. I must tell you that you were rejected for going to the Soviet Union to study. The Party and the Youth Organization consider you politically unreliable. I think you made some mistakes along the way, and in your papers you answered that your social background is petty bourgeois, that finished you off. You are an excellent student and if it was up to me, you would go, sorry."

My anxiety about being able to get into college got
really grew. Years later I laughed at my devastation at the
time and was very happy I had been denied that privilege.
Much later I became the boss of some of these Moscow
University graduates. They were frequently trained in
narrow in specialties with huge gaps in theoretical and
general knowledge. I think utilitarian compartmentalization
was the reason. After a short "apprenticeship" in the
technical area for which they were supposedly trained, they
were transferred and given administrative positions in order
to climb the bureaucratic ladder.

My continuing, inability to master Polish writing,
grammar and spelling gave use to further development. The
teacher, when looking at my compositions, would sit in
silence, in utter exasperation, not knowing how to react.
She could not understand how a seemingly intelligent boy
was unable to squeeze out half a page of some decent
writing; sometimes the stuff I submitted was beyond the
range of assessment. Nothing could be said; there was no
quality in it at all, just a heap of mistakes and nonsense.
Not that I spoke a foreign language. Polish should have
been considered my native tongue. The situation became so
critical that Mrs. Falkowska had the idea of accepting Ed

Buttermilk into the orphanage. He lived away from his hamlet in a boarding house and jumped at the chance to live with us for free in exchange for preparing me for the maturity exam, a big deal in Europe, without passing them there was no college career. The final month before these exams passed in furious preparations under relentless and grueling language exercises conducted by Ed. I thought I was under double jeopardy, my political unreliability and that cursed Polish language.

The fateful day finally arrived and I went to the exams as if mounting a scaffold. Little did I know that the situation was not that simple. I was mostly an A student in all other subjects. The Polish teacher therefore had a stake in not creating the impression that a strong average B+ student was unable to acquire rudimentary skills in the Polish language under her instruction. She hovered around my exam station most of the time giving me a little helping hand, not too much, not doing anything illegal, just providing a little oversight. I knew then that I had a chance. When I came before the table where the exam board sat to hand out the diplomas, the Chairman said:

'Sven, we had a tough time with you, but the vote was to pass you, only because of your other grades, and we hope you will be forced to learn Polish in college and in life. Good luck."

On to College

I applied to the Polytechnic in the ancient city of Wroclaw (Known before the war by its German name, Breslau) where they had an Aeronautical Department. The competition was fierce, ten candidates for each opening. It was during the application process that the communist version of affirmative action entered into play. After the written exams there was an interview, which was usually decisive, regardless of the results of the written exam and in spite of their being officially declared as all-important. Moments like these one never forgets.

"Mr. Sonnenberg, tell us a little about yourself. About your family background, where do you come from to us, and why you want to be an aeronautical engineer? There are so many other occupations, which will let you serve the Socialist Fatherland.

The first and last questions were open traps. The middle one was my salvation. I fudged a little bit on the first one giving my father as being a traveling salesman hoping that they did not have my Soviet application. The second was a savior because of the orphanage; six years of indoctrination, no family influence anymore, the chances that I could turn into a loyal guy after all. With the third question I did not do too well, but passed. Instead of proudly announcing that I had technical aptitudes and wanted to work in aeronautics for the good of Socialism, I was close enough by saying that I wanted to contribute to the Polish aircraft industry.

I was admitted! The orphanage tried to outfit me as best they could for my journey into life. I got some new clothes, the distinguishing feature of which was a cap with a very large brim that my friends from college remember and make fun of at every reunion. I also got a very small suitcase in which three items rattled around, a loaf of bread, a round cheese and my compass set. Among the freshmen, all coming from proper homes, I must have looked like a strange bird indeed in my poorly fitting clothes, each piece from a different outfit. Our aeronautical studies began in front of the old and impressive University building. The freshmen class was collected there in a large group. An announcement was made that there was a need to sell books to the city population. The instructions were to form troikas, spontaneously pick up the allocated books and go and sell them. I stood there looking around, not knowing what to do. One student came over to me and asked if I wanted to form a team with him. That is how I met Joe with whom I created a lifelong bond. I was cringing at the prospect of going from door to door in the designated district, peddling communist propaganda books. I can clearly recall the discomfort of knocking on doors and trying to push Lenin's trash on people. The initiation over, I felt pride and happiness mixed with awe walking the halls of that renowned old institution.

The seeds of tragedy had been sown for many right at that exam interview, at the affirmative action gate. After the first semester tests the class stratified. A distinctive group of underachievers emerged. These were mostly peasants or the vaunted proletariat kids who got in because of the points given for proper social backgrounds. The faculty was composed of old fiercely demanding prewar professors and they totally dismissed the progressive idea of promoting the proletariat offspring and giving them favorable treatment. The professors were "brutal" and no one could do anything about it. They actually did not like and were silently opposed to any manipulation and demanded performance. This was of course at odds with the Party's political goals. In response, the all-important ZMP youth organization came up with the idea to pair the performers with those less able to cope.

"Colleague Sven, your assignment in the group will be to help and be responsible for colleague Pytlasz. You will see to it that he gets passing grades, moves along toward finishing college and applies himself. We will arrange a separate room for both of you, and you will report on colleague Pytlasz's progress at our meetings."

So, I got a comfortable room on the upper floor of a convent building, but the price for that was a Sisyphean effort to pull colleague Pytlasz along. He was a diligent and good fellow. He kneeled every morning and evening at his bed and said his prayers, sometimes aloud, asking God to give him strength and ability. That, God did not grant him. He flunked out after two years of mental torment. But that was when I was no longer in charge; nevertheless I pitied those guys because some of them desperately wanted to achieve; somehow the mental capacity was not there. Only a limited number of them finished college, and all strictly on merit, some were real achievers not needing affirmative action in the first place.

This is not to say that peasant or proletarian backgrounds were mental impediments to higher education, it simply testifies that government meddling in natural processes is counterproductive or disastrous. The Party's efforts were not so much a desire to compensate for past wrongs when only the well-to-do could afford college, but rather a need to create its own loyal intellectual elite, faithful to the Party. That backfired badly. Over the years the educated sons of workers noticed that their own further progress was severely curtailed, they could not earn to their capacity, their children had difficulty getting into college because now they no longer were pure proletarians. What these children had to do was go to work at the lowest menial jobs for two to three years, as bricklayers or such, in order to attain the right status and then qualify. What is more, the new elite started clustering in the better neighborhoods and took special interest in improving the schools for their kids. Suddenly the Party was faced with exactly the situation it had tried to eliminate. An elite more interested in self-improvement, hostile to the Party's meddling in private life and yearning for freedom from the shackles imposed by the political system. What ingratitude!!!. Judge Clarence Thomas comes to mind.

My college years were tumultuous and memorable. I got a stipend and a dormitory room; this was just enough for me not to starve. I qualified for all this because of my complete and utter state of poverty and lack of a family to give me any sort of support. The only thing I had to do was maintain my grades in the B+ range, which I did with great zeal and not only to keep my stipend. If I failed to do that, there was no mercy. Before I landed in the general college dormitory I lived in a Jewish boarding house called "Bursa;" it was run by some Jewish organization jointly with the state. This was where destitute kids without any family and too old for the orphanage ended up after high school when they attended college or got jobs, or were in trade schools. For three months I was there and, very unhappy. The activists, and there was a plethora of them of different shades of red or with unclear political agendas, constantly organizing sociopolitical meetings. I felt lost in that highly charged intellectual environment— a bunch of Jewish besserwissers (know-it-alls) pulling me every which way. I was non-religious, politically nondescript and all I wanted was to study aeronautics, not much else mattered. I soon became a loner a sort of outcast. I finally applied for the general dormitory, which was almost exclusively filled

with pure Polish guys. I immediately found a group I was comfortable with, and after the semester ended and new dormitory arrangements were being made, Joe, the guy I met during the book sale, proposed sharing a room. There were four of us, and we formed a very close group that stayed together all six years. Joe Lewalski a medium-height guy of non-descript hair color somewhat resembling James Dean, Adam Borowski, also of medium height, but extremely skinny, so skinny that when a draft pushed a door open and no one entered the room, it was said that it must have been Adam. Adam was a chain smoker. Peter (Przemyslaw) Krol was the tallest with a baby face and blond hair, blue eyes and what seemed to be too much of a liking for alcohol. I looked like a Jew. Short, dark with a protruding nose, slightly deformed head and, surprise, surprise, green eyes. Of vital importance and of consuming concern to each of us was our individual standing with girls. We tried to explore that, so that we knew and could support each other in that area as best we could. Peter provoked strong reactions in women; he was liked or rejected, and when disliked, it was strong dislike at first sight. Peter usually brought in the ugliest girl he could find. We said, "Peter what is it with you, that girl stinks!"
Peter:

"That is my choice, you guys, understand? I have to show those haughty bitches [in the female dormitory] that in my eyes they do not amount to anything."

"O.K. Peter, O.K."

Joe, in spite of a certain handsomeness, did not have very good luck with girls. Every relationship he began was sort of forced and unsatisfactory. He was the wittiest of us all, with a great sense of humor—jolly good company. Adam, by my guess, should have been unattractive to girls. They were not falling over themselves for him, but there were certain types of women who would latch onto Adam and would not let go. That was the case with Madame Lis, a very cute redhead who pursued him relentlessly. We had to help Adam escape when she showed up since Adam was not interested. Adam was mostly indifferent to all that hoopla with the girls. He listened to our frustrations and smiled gently as if saying, "Fools, what is all this fuss about?" Adam later married Wanda, and we pitied him. As for me, I was pathologically shy around girls, and my dating scene, well…there wasn't any. I did not think that there was a girl in the world who would want me. That changed when I started dating Cynthia, and I fell madly in love and did not care much about other girls. My three friends took great care in helping me along, doing everything they could to promote that relationship. They were most considerate. We married after I graduated. That marriage ended after five unhappy years, I was about to say, five years too many, but without that ordeal I would surely not have met Elizabeth, a unique and very attractive woman. She was unique not only because she endured me for thirty-six years and probably would have continued had she not been cut down by cancer, but because of the unusual combination of qualities she possessed. Qualities, I will most certainly never find again. Of course, I have written a separate essay about her.

Joe had an artistic talent, he could capture scenes on paper, and I still have some of his drawings from that time. In our class there was a woman, a bit older than any of us. She was not pretty at all, but had amazing sex appeal. The pull she exerted was strong, we were at a loss to explain it, and some of us were quite crazy about her; her name was Stacey Domin. One day Joe said,

"Hey guys, I need to dampen your enthusiasm a little bit."

He showed us an impressively executed drawing of an old, wrinkled and naked woman with a crucifix necklace between her long hanging breasts.

"That is how she will look not too long from now."

Eventually Ludwig got her, for a while at least, and we were happy for Ludwig, but very envious.

The bond that had developed between us was as strong as the best family ties could be. Now, what about anti-Semitism? During that time and until 1952-53 it was strictly forbidden, and I felt it only in a very subtle way from guys showing an unfriendly attitude and avoiding my company. That did not bother me in the least because I had my group, which was dubbed the "kolkhoz" by others for the way we shared between us the meager resources we had. If there was a date, the dating guy would take the one suit we had, and the best shoes, and the others would wait it out in bed. My kolkhoz guys were totally devoid of any traces of anti-Semitism, and our relationships developed into lifelong bonds, especially between Joe and me. Feeling the comfort of mutual support, we settled in for the bumpy ride that was college life.

The Ride

We had to deal with two fully loaded aspects of academic life during those times. One obviously was learning. The professorship was the old prewar cadre and mostly apolitical or hostile to communism, as there were no others available as yet. Besides, these professors wanted to maintain the impression of how tough the aeronautical department was—a little bit of self-promotion. We were the marines of the college army and others viewed us with respect mixed with pity for our cruel fate. We were viewed as an elite suffering awful academic hardship for the privilege. The professors maintained the prewar atmosphere of Wilno University, where they all had taught but which no longer belonged to Poland having been incorporated into the Soviet Union. They addressed us as Mister in defiance of the official push to use Colleague or Comrade. They showed old-fashioned courtesy to students, mixed with steely demands and a reverence for the students who excelled, viewing them as the hope for the continuation of their own work. That lasted a full two years, years we later remembered with nostalgia. Then in 1953 the government decided that they had too many prospective aeronautical engineers on their hands. The decision was announced that the department was going to be dissolved and about fifty percent of us would transfer to Warsaw, the capital city. The selection process began once again, amidst high anxiety, because most of us were crazy about aeronautics. So, social backgrounds started to play a role again. In addition to our academic standing, our personal files traveled with us and they were getting bigger by the day, filled with all kinds of tidbits, valid information intermixed with malicious stuff often intended to do harm. There was a student who was an undeniable genius; his name was Podhorski-Okolow—a double name denoting an aristocratic heritage (which he tried in vain to hide by using only the last part). I envied his mathematical prowess and he was close to my group and me. In spite of his show of political correctness he was not chosen. The hourglass of our bitterness against the system started flowing toward the bottom. We wondered though, how he did get in, in the first place; someone must have been blinded by his A+ grades from top to bottom. The kolkhoz bunch all ended up in Warsaw. All of us had fuzzy (but not prohibitive) social backgrounds. What helped me again were my many years without adverse societal connections (confined to an orphanage and select politically controlled schools). We all were in good academic standing, and we were all politically correct, sort of. That is how our four-year odyssey in Warsaw began.

Alongside the academic stuff, we had to deal with the political activity of the ZMP—the youth organization. Membership was a hundred percent. Only some older students were in the Party, very few. These were postwar times, and so a few older guys, in their thirties, were in our college as well a few who had survived the war in the Soviet Union. These Soviet groomees were especially fierce and devoted. Every two weeks we had meetings to review past events in school, and to discuss and deal with deviations from the Party line in personal behavior and speech. One designated member of the group would prepare a short political presentation on the latest outrage Imperialist America had committed or on some select interpretation of Lenin's or Stalin's works. We were also a large number of ready to mobilize bodies when needed. All the Party authorities had to do was go to the dormitory in the evening and sequester everybody, organize groups and send them out on assignments. The one or two memorable events come to mind.

The Polish parliament, which at that time was already a rubber stamp for Party directives, decided to nationalize the last vestiges of private enterprise, the small retail stores including the pharmacies. They passed the measure in a secret session late in the day, and an inventory was to take place that night nationwide. The organizers of that inventory came to the dormitory with police teams. We were again divided into troikas, a policeman was assigned to each and off we went to take inventory. It was a cold late afternoon in winter; we took a streetcar (they were running until midnight) to the designated store and started the inventory [4]. A few hours into it we got tired and hungry and the policeman offered to get us some food. He brought sandwiches; we did not ask from where and gobbled them down. By four o'clock in the morning we had completed enough of the inventory to assure that the owner, now temporarily made an employee of the state, could be held accountable if some major item got moved out of the store. These stores had been family businesses for generations and overnight the owners received nothing, but a pitiful salary. To add insult to injury, they were now responsible

---

[4] Joe, whom I asked to verify my memory, insists that this event took place in Wroclaw. He says that we were working on the inventory of ladies underwear and adds with a mischievous smile that only I blushed while counting bras and panties.

for the upkeep and accountable for the property and its contents. At four o'clock in the morning we started trudging through deep snow back to the dormitory, which was a few miles away. No streetcars running yet. We soon discovered that the sandwiches we had eaten were spoiled; they began their work and it was thorough. Every few yards or so we had to squat in the snow, the freezing wind howling against our bare behinds. We left a dense trail on the sidewalks and everywhere else in what should have been taken as an expression of our opinion about that nationalization. We quickly got over that terribly unpleasant incident and went back to our other worries and joys; nevertheless another small heap of little grains of bitterness accumulated in the hourglass.

During summer vacations, we were sometimes compelled to go and help with the harvest. The Polish countryside was fragmented into very inefficient and predominantly backward family farms. The Polish peasant had a fascination with land ownership and the land was divided for generation among sons over and over until the resulting tiny farms were not sustainable. The Party on the other hand had a fascination with collectivization, Soviet style. The Soviet collectivization under Stalin was unspeakably brutal, and the peasants that were promised the land confiscated from the landed gentry got it initially and then were robbed of it by forced collectivization, that is, they became state workers on land previously owned by them, that land then being made into huge enterprises called kolkhozes. The idea behind this was not so much to improve the efficiency of agriculture, but to eradicate all private ownership and gain total control of the peasantry, who, if they remained private owners, would constitute a class difficult to deal with, unpredictable. The Polish Communist Party longed for collectivization, but decided that this would only be a bloody and messy operation in the face of the peasantry's fierce attachment to the land. What they did, however was to establish large estate farms run by the state from land confiscated from displaced German landowners or carved from huge Polish aristocratic estates. These were called PGR (State Agricultural Farms). These farms were supposed to be models to show the peasantry how well things could be run and maybe with time, slowly, achieve a milder road to the elimination of private property without using Stalin's methods. It turned out that these farms were an unmitigated disaster. Crops were not harvested, equipment rusted, theft was rampant. So was mismanagement. We were sent to these farms to harvest crops, while the workers who were supposed to do it cheered us on with sarcasm and contempt.

So, we arrived at Von Bodeck's, a former German estate in what once was East Prussia, now given to Poland as compensation for the Soviets' seizure of a good chunk of southeastern Poland. It was already getting dark when we arrived by horse-drawn wagon, ten of us. In the dusk we could clearly see the Von Bodeck name in big letters in stone on top of the arched entrance gate. By the time we found the manager it was already dark; we had obviously woken him up. Disheveled, he took a kerosene lamp and led us to a large building.

"This is where you will stay.
We looked around; not much could be seen in the light of the kerosene lamp.

"Any place to sleep here? We have been up and traveling all day."

"You can sleep in the ballroom, it is sufficiently large for all of you. You can go to the barn and get some straw, I will show you where. By the way, you will start work at six. You have to be ready at five thirty to be taken to the fields."

And so it was, we got the straw and next day we arranged it across half of the ballroom. In the daylight, we could appreciate the Von Bodeck mansion. It could have been the set of "Dynasty", with a central stairway ascending from the large hall. The whole building was completely empty and swept clean. The windows were intact but none of the facilities were working, no water, and no functioning toilet. There was no toilet anywhere, period. We had to go out in the night into the magnificent park surrounding the mansion. What a mess, at least by the end of our two-month stay. My job in the field was cutting the wheat. This was done according to an age-old tradition of a team with scythes cutting down swathes of wheat with a rhythmic motion of the hand-held implement. This called for a repetitive movement of the waist for at least eight hours a day with a half hour break for lunch. After a day of such labor the city slickers fell dead on the floor not able to raise an arm. This is not to say that Von Bodeck lacked machinery, but every single machine was broken and unusable.

Once, in the middle of the night when we were dreaming of those rhythmic motions, dead tired, the manager came running in and, tearing at each of us, woke us up, shouting,

> "Get up, get up, two colts fell into the sewage pit, they are drowning! I will be fired if they perish, I need help."

We dragged ourselves out to the sewage pit, which was filled with the runoff from the pig sty and whatever other waste was around. In dim kerosene lamplight we could see two colts trashing around in the pool of that choking, stinking brew. The hell with the manager—but we could not let those two frightened animals perish! We set to work. With slings and bars we tried to heave them out, but the more strategies we tried the more panicky the animals became. The situation grew critical, and the only way we could save them, it seemed, was to lower some of us into the brew and somehow pass a sling under the animals bellies and haul them out. We got them out by some miracle. We did not go to work that day; it was devoted to washing, using the cold well water. We stank for the remaining two weeks although we washed and washed and washed.

We all came back sick. Jerry was really sick and stayed in bed. We made a collection and bought a few bottles of expensive Benedictine. We were sure that that choice alcoholic beverage, purportedly invented by medieval monks for keeping them in health, was the ultimate cure for any illness, but Jerry grew weaker by the day. On the forth day we decided to take him to the hospital, with two of us supporting him under his arms to get him to the taxi. It was pneumonia and he barely came out of it. That experience certainly made us dismiss the pervasive propaganda about the achievements of the PGR enterprises. Slowly and irrevocably the more thoughtful of us ceased to believe anything anymore. This led the more curious and concerned to search out information from sources other than the government media. Radio Free Europe became some of the sources, but that is another story.

Before we left Wroclaw I witnessed a scene that etched itself into my memory. I was doing some chores in the (ZMP) office in the University building. Adjacent to the room I was in was the office of the Chairman. A student came in and left the door ajar, and I heard him asking for an application to join the Youth Organization. The Chairman started asking him some preliminary questions about his family, what his father did, et cetera,

"Where are you from?"

"Katowice." (A heavily ethnic German part of Poland)

"Were you there when the Germans held the area?"

"Yes,"

"Then you probably were a member of the Hitlerjugend."

"Yes."

A few other questions followed. The guy was admitted and later I saw him moving up in the organization. At the time I was stunned; it seemed so strange that I, with my bourgeois background, had so much trouble, always under suspicion and tolerated only because of my orphanage past, and here is this guy with Hitlerjugend training and no problems! The significance of that incident I understood years later. You always accept a good man from the competition with open arms!

Our kolhoz group intact arrived in Warsaw together with the others who had been selected in Wroclaw, that year 1953. We grew even closer now, sharing our intimate thoughts (considered a fatal flaw during those times), but we had an absolute and idealistic confidence in each other.

There were still the four of us, Adam, Joe (Zdzislaw), Peter (Przemyslaw) and I. There was no one like us in the university, and the legend continued. We were consummately supportive of each other and that was evident and visible to all. Each excelled in an academic discipline, Adam became the darling of the structures professor and Joe excelled in very difficult spatial geometry and so on, I was the darling of the electrical department head. We therefore had protectors. The worst off of the group was Peter—a "know-it-all" smart alec. We had to keep a close watch on his academic performance, and that was my elected job—prefect of the kolkhoz police, they called me. When term projects were due the three of us labored late into the night to finish it for Peter, while he himself was supplying beer and rolls and fussing over the details, "No, no, no, this is not going to work!"

I had a couple of protectors, but one powerful enemy. This was Professor Niemand, a Jew and a former divisional commissar of the Red Army. It could not have been worse. The guy hated me. Unfortunately for me, I got the hiccups in the middle of his lecture. He thought this was done on purpose to mock him.

"Comrade Sonnenberg (not mister—he was after all
a commissar), I demand that you stop or leave the
room."

"Professor, I cannot help it, I am sorry, but I cannot
leave the room, the lecture is too valuable to me."

This provoked an angry comment, which I do not
remember, but I did not leave the room. Again, like in high
school, he was unable to harm me too badly, because I
knew his subject too well and he could not justify any
action against me before the other professor who held me in
high esteem.

We were academically strong, but that was only the
half of it. Into play came political standing. And here a
strange thing happened. We performed all the required
duties demanded from loyal students of the regime with
some intelligence and skill, but with a twist. We were
unorthodox, we openly read marginally acceptable
literature like Rabelais, but not the outright forbidden stuff,
we initiated controversial discussions, and maintained not
very kosher associations with people considered politically
unreliable or hostile. When called on the carpet for this, the
simple and disarming answer was, "we are working on-so-
and-so to bring him to our side." The forbidden stuff, like

Orwell, we read in absolute secrecy with the door key turned and left in. We craved to listen to Radio Free Europe, but that was difficult and very dangerous; expulsion and a note in the perpetrator's personal file that would travel with him forever would follow if caught. We were watched, tolerated with exasperation and getting away with a lot. That created a situation where the intellectually curious and somewhat politically volatile elements gravitated to us. That way we had a comet tail of the friends of the Kolkhoz behind us, some were colorful individuals indeed.

Nicos Karalis.

Nicos was a Greek Royal Air Force captain with a facial profile taken from the ancient art on the Grecian vases seen in museums. He had black eyes and pitch-black hair. He was rather short and on the heavy side. His guitar made up for these physical shortcomings. The ladies melted to the sound of his nostalgic songs. During the war he flew Lancaster bombers in the British Royal Air Force. He joined the Greek Communist Party in Greece after WWII and fought in Marcos' communist uprising in Greece. After that was squashed he escaped to communist Poland with a host of others like him. Nicos decided on an aeronautical education in line with his previous occupation, and began to study with us. The Greek government put a death sentence on him if captured or if he came back to Greece. The partisan commander upon dissolving his unit in Poland asked the women, also in the unit, to line up opposite his men and ordered, "Forward march." When the two lines came together facing each other the commander said,

> "The comrades facing each other are now pronounced man and wife, good luck to each of you."

That is how Nicos married Kula, a disciplined Party member. The marriage turned into an unmitigated disaster, but this was a bit later. In the meantime we befriended Nicos, who was a gifted guitar player and a fantastic storyteller. He was very serious about his political convictions, but they were not his life's passion. He was a sex maniac, and I have never met anyone that passionate about sex since Nicos. He was much older, had vast experience in that area and thought his duty was to educate us, greenhorns. The extent of his obsession can be illustrated by the following incident. I was walking with Nicos to a lecture; we passed a ladies' bathhouse. In those days people still went to public bathhouses to take a shower. Nothing devious about that, many did not have bathrooms in their houses. Nicos turned to me and said,

"I would love to be a wall in that shower room so I could hear all the shh…shh… in the toilet nearby, it is music to my ears."

We loved Nicos, his cooking was great, his stories most exciting and his guitar a delight. One day I met my friend Jacob in the street, and we stopped for a chat. Jacob:

"I finally met your much-talked about Nicos, he is a painful idiot."

"Why?"

"I invited him for lunch, and we waited God knows how long to be served. Finally the waiter came and was rude. And you know what Nicos started lecturing me about?"

"What?"

"He said that this was a very clear evidence of the superiority of the Socialist system over Capitalism. In Capitalism the waiter would bow and be abjectly subservient, here he retains his pride."

We had a talk about this with Nicos and asked him not to bring shame to us again by such stupidity, which by

association could ruin our reputation. Shortly after that
Nicos started avoiding us. Three of us cornered him and
asked what the matter was.

> Nicos: "My friends, a disaster has befallen me, I
> was thrown out of the Party and I am a leper now.
> It is dangerous for you to associate with me and
> show any signs of friendship, so stay away."

First, we fell to the floor with laughter upon seeing
his somber and dejected demeanor. When we pulled
ourselves together, we warmly congratulated him and went
to drown his sorrow in cheap alcohol. We never delved into
the reasons; it had to happen sooner or later. Nicos'
conduct in life and the Party were totally at odds. Somehow
he had made a terrible turn in his life and joined that
criminal cabal when he did not have to and had no reason
to in the world. Maybe he had an idiotic nodule in his brain
somewhere after all. He recovered nicely from that
expulsion with jolly help from us. Nicos had a son by Kula
named Fedon and after Nicos and Kula divorced she moved
to a commune established by those noble fighters for the
happiness of mankind, remnants of the communist rebellion
in Greece. Nicos visited his son and started courting Katina
a teacher in the commune. On one of the visits he was
summoned to the local Party executive.

"Comrade Nicos, we have a delicate matter to discuss with you. We can see that you are getting serious about comrade Katina. We have grown concerned, because we think she is not suitable for you, a respected comrade. You see, to put it delicately, she sees a lot of men."

"Comrades, I must tell you that I would never, ever consider an inexperienced woman for a wife."

(Getting a little bold having been around us for a while, eh.

That settled the matter and Nicos married Katina. It became an outstanding marriage. We liked Katina a lot and enjoyed being invited into their flat for social events. On one of the visits to see Fedon Kula put him up in a tree and erected a manure ring around it to symbolically deny Nicos access to his beloved son. Nicos became so upset that he died of a heart attack shortly after, at age 49 and never saw his beloved Greece again

Ludwig Natkaniec

Ludwig was a fellow of medium height with a freckled complexion and reddish blond hair. He had a smiling, broad face, and his distinguishing feature was the large gap between his two front teeth. Very mild-mannered and easygoing he used to come by, drink a bit and mostly listen in silence to our ravings about things as we took the world apart. It happened that the Youth Organization (the ZMP, to which we all belonged) announced a campaign to improve our grades, a noble cause. At one of the meetings I got up, asked to say something. I arduously avoided any public speaking since my shyness was pathological. This time, though, I got up and said,

> "Colleagues, I think we need to fundamentally change our attitudes. We should not just study for the sake of passing grades; we need to hunger for knowledge and aim for the highest grades and ease up a little bit on chasing girls. I know some of us are barely doing enough to get a passing C. This attitude was expressed to me by colleague Natkaniec."

Ludwig became a whipping boy. Not a meeting passed without his name being mentioned and dragged through mud. He became public enemy No. 1. I was shocked and frightened about having harmed his graduation chances. I literally went on my knees to ask forgiveness from Ludwig for my stupidity. I could clearly feel the pain of that anguished English colonel in the story "The Bridge over the River Kwai." I also said to myself "My God, what have I done". Slowly the furor subsided and Ludwig went on with his studies and graduated. It is now half a century since these events took place, and I am still bitterly ashamed of my action. Ludwig forgave me and became a devoted friend. I worked with him very closely for years when he became a company test pilot, enormously successful and universally liked. During the times of trouble, in 1968 when I was under the political whip, he went out of his way to protect me, with considerable danger to himself. Ludwig died at the age of 65 in retirement; the air force flew in formation over his funeral procession to show respect and admiration for their beloved fellow pilot.

That incident more than any other opened my eyes, to the evil nature of the communist movement (and for that matter to any "isms" especially the contemporary run away liberalism). The mark of their "morality" was betrayal, hypocritical adherence to the Party line of the day and unquestioned obedience to it. The infamous public self-criticism sessions were the abject and cringingly humiliating expressions of that. It is known that Party members would condemn themselves to harsh punishment or even death by confessing to nonexistent "crimes" against the state or movement without torture or the least pressure, simply on the notion that the Party needed it now for its lofty noble ends. The Orwellian vision became reality, parents had to talk in secret from their kids, and every utterance in all circumstances had to be weighed for its political consequences (check the US universities now) and remember Pavlik Morozov [3.] After the Ludwig incident we became doubly cautious in our speech. My kolkhoz fellows tried to soothe me as best they could when they saw my inconsolable grief.

Roman Ptak

Roman was a tall fellow one or two years older than I, that means about three years older than the average student. He was dashingly handsome with a protruding chin denoting energy and courage. Bright blue eyes beaming wit added an irresistible finish to his appearance aiding in the seduction of ladies. Roman came to Poland from France, the son of emigrants impoverished and out of work in prewar depressed Poland, who had left Poland for work in the French coal mines. In France Roman was an unruly youngster and his reasons for coming to the Soviet block were somewhat obscure. He was received in Poland well, a propaganda piece by his mere presence—the sons and daughters of the proletariat returning to the fold of the socialist fatherland. Roman gave lip service to the whole whirlwind of the Party and ZMP with their constant demands for some sort of political expression, meetings, imperialist condemnation rallies and so forth. He put a sarcastic smile on his face for these activities. He was street smart and experienced, and concentrated on enjoying life, keeping busy seducing ladies and playing cards. He was one of those gifted guys who could, with a minimum effort it seemed, absorb the necessary knowledge to get passing grades. Sometimes though he got into trouble, and this is where we would intervene.

"Roman, you lazy bum, get up from that bed, there's a lecture today you can't afford to miss!"

"You fellows should be more understanding. I am trying hard to combat my laziness and I sit up ready to move, but then my internal struggle comes to a pitch and I fall back exhausted."

Roman viewed us, the Kolkhoz guys, as a bunch of interesting jackasses not yet well versed in the intricacies of life. Sure, we all had a life goal, we wanted to become outstanding engineers, but that for Roman was not an end in itself. He liked to immerse himself from time to time in the charged atmosphere of our free- wheeling discussions, where one could safely say things that were very dangerous elsewhere. He also didn't mind benefiting from little favors like a loan for a card game and some food if we had it. We shook our heads over Roman. The ease and smoothness he displayed moving through life, his carefree appearance, dazzled us. We worried, worked long hours, and were concerned about issues. Not Roman, the little all-knowing smirk never left his face. Roman escaped from Poland early, at the first opportunity after graduation. He went back to France and became wealthy. Now, half a century later, we have renewed contact. He lives half the year in Florida in a beautiful house, an estate rather, and is a happy-go-lucky fellow like he was in the old days; for me he is like a little ray of sun coming through occasionally in my lonely retirement. Whenever we, the other guys, get together we never fail to remember him from the old days—ahh… Roman. The benefit to us, among others things from knowing Roman during the student days, was that he added a good measure of skepticism and sarcasm to our slowly developing hatred of the communist system and displayed before us a lifestyle we could not attain.

It so happened that when I was writing these lines a call came in from Roman—now in Florida. His voice was full of panic,

"What is the matter with these American women? The other day I spoke to a lady in the shopping center just to make some conversation, I need to improve my English. She treated me as if I was going to rape her right there and then. It is my impression that their minds got terribly screwed up, it is so unlike France where women still know their place."

My reply was:

"Roman, you have to know that the present American culture forged by the feminist movement and media considers all males as potential rapists and abject abusers. So, don't touch an American female if you do not want to rot in an American jail."

I have to add that Roman is endowed with pheromone glands. These glands at the base of the nose have a powerful and irresistible pull on females. He never in his life had the slightest trouble with women—they flocked to him without exception and that as is true for every man who has those glands. Roman's pheromones are mighty. He sat one evening in an entertainment bar (not in America). He was alone at the table. When the gorgeous singer finished her number, she came down from the stage to mingle with the guests. She circled around and stopped at Roman's table.

"May I sit down?"

"Certainly!"

"I need a lover for tonight, would you be available?"

"But of course".

This is how their liaison began. As time went on it became somewhat bizarre and I will stop here because Roman may come across this writing—he may resent me telling the rest of the story.

We had a number of other associates. Though colorful, they are still in our memories, but the details have faded. The whole environment we had created by our personalities was devoid of any racial overtones. Greek, Jew or Frenchman, it did not matter in the least and never came up. The student body was fairly homogenous, mostly pure Poles with these few exceptions. It was the mark of our group that these tiny minorities gravitated to us to find a comfortable environment. The Nicos' did not find friends among those whom we suspected of harboring hidden animosities toward Jews or others considered not very pure Poles. Unfortunately it was again the majority who displayed indifference and lofty separateness. I could not have cared less. I had my friends and the comet tail behind the Kolkhoz and that was just fine. Overt anti-Semitism was absolutely forbidden and did not appear. We had little contact with the "outside" world, being confined to our dormitories and academia, and that also helped us to forget about that ugly national trait. We also did not know much of what was happening in society at large, the arrests, disappearances, and not-very- public persecutions.

Official anti-Semitic rumblings started in Poland in 1951-52, and came out of the Soviet Union, just before Stalin's death. Until then we were not aware that the Soviet Party has started anti-Jewish actions as early as 1948. It took some time to get the campaign going full speed. In the meantime they murdered a few prominent Jewish artists there and arrested others. Poland had not yet joined the action. It really went into high gear in the whole Soviet block with the announcement that a group of doctors who had treated the highest echelon of the Soviet government,

Stalin included, had been poisoning them for a long time. These doctors were mostly Jews, so it was an organized Jewish-Zionist anti-communist plot, and they all confessed that that was so. For a while the tense atmosphere around the Jews grew. "They are the silent sneaky enemies of communism, burrowing deep and cleverly undermining the most vital centers of our society." The atmosphere changed overnight. It was O.K. to hate the Jews again and fear for our safety grew. After Stalin's death it took some time before it was announced that the doctors were innocent and no plot had existed. I remember Mrs. Falkowska's reaction; she was now in Warsaw and lectured in one of the Party-affiliated schools.

"Thank God it turned out that way. Otherwise we would all have been in trouble. (Sic)"

In spite of the end of the "doctors affair," official anti-Semitism had now taken hold under the guise of anti-Zionism. I felt the general situation changing in society, but for a while it did not affect me so much personally, that is, there was no change in my immediate environment. Besides Mrs. Falkowska there was also Ms. Milstein, who taught Marxism-Leninism at the Polytechnic, a compulsory subject that had to be passed every year. Both Mrs. Falkowska and Ms. Milstein from the days of the orphanage continued to take an interest in our welfare. Dinners every week in Ms. Milstein's one-room flat became routine events for me. I was not very comfortable with that care, but not too disturbed either. This was a contact with the old communist guard who supposedly knew what was brewing, and the dinners were nothing to be dismissive about for a starving student. The tensions though between Mrs. Milstein and me grew steadily, mainly from her side. She became increasingly angry with my probing questions, doubts and cynicism about communism. She nevertheless maintained the dinner schedule faithfully. And then came the Twenties Party congress in February 1956 where Khrushev denounced Stalin and ridiculed him for his conduct during the war, saying that he planned military campaigns on a rotating globe in his cabinet. This was read at a supposedly confidential meeting, at which Ms. Milstein was present. The room was greatly amused and burst into sarcastic laughter at some points during the solemn reading. Ms. Milstein stood up and shouted,

> "Why are you laughing? Have you no shame! Such a tragedy! Such a tragedy!"

Her world collapsed. I felt a little sadness for her. But everything in my world had already collapsed long ago. For me it was incredible that such a system, with a tyrant at the top, could now be denounced so easily by the very same who supported it for such a long time. How could it be that youngsters like me, fiercely indoctrinated would in a relatively short time see the rottenness of that movement while the Milsteins could not, in almost a life time, even with their closest friends disappearing, murdered and tortured. How could that be? But then I must remind myself of some contemporaries, nothing will budge a believing soul, for every evil committed there is a rationalization. Woeful human nature! As far as the revelations of crimes and atrocities, I knew a little bit about them already, as to the rest, I figured it out. In October 1956, after Khrushchev's revelation, another crucial event in the communist education of the young (and not so young) generation took place. That was the suppression by Soviet tanks of the Hungarian anti-communist uprising. Here I will turn the narrative over to Joe, who reminded me of just that event. He relates:

It was October 1956 when I found myself in a Warsaw streetcar with colleagues going from the University to the dormitory. It was just after the anti-

*communist uprising in Budapest. With us was a student
who had recently returned from Budapest. We clustered
around him, listening to the stories he brought back from
there. The guy started to shake as he began to describe a
lull in the fighting during which hundreds of hungry people
formed a long line in front of a bakery in his neighborhood.
They had learned that the backer had somehow managed
miraculously to bake some bread. Suddenly a Soviet tank
came around the corner at high speed and ran over the
whole line, steering so that he got fifty or so people. I will
never forget the reaction of one of our colleagues named
Oleksiak. He was a quiet guy, very talented and most
gentle. One could imagine him as a monk working
diligently in some monastery, totally absorbed, designing
the fancy letters for Guttenberg's Bible. When the narrator
finished there was a dead silence for a while and then
Oleksiak said, "Now, that was really a piggish thing to
do." That understatement made us all burst into laughter,
but when it died down we parted, to carry this story deep
within us to this day. It made the rounds of the university
and perhaps more than any other atrocity sank, in because
of Oleksiak and his remark. I thought then, "If this is the
way you bastards are trying to bring happiness to mankind,
screw yourselves! I am as far from you as I can be." It is*

scary to think that I could have wound up being an armchair leftist as described below. See addendum C, my letter to Joe and his description of the ponytail guy.

There had been a rash of suicides among the old communist cadre, and one day the police called me out from work, asking if I had the key to comrade Milstein's apartment. I went with the police to the flat to find Ms. Milstein dead on the floor in the bathroom with the gas turned on. The smell in the staircase had alerted the neighbors and they called the Police. It was ruled a suicide, although the speculation was that there might have been foul play by someone involved in her prewar communist activities.

The whole anti-Jewish official attitude took a turn for the worse after the Suez Canal war, when Israel in alliance with France and England fought the Arabs. This was the year 1957, and I was graduating from College. I had a final run-in with the commissar, comrade Niemand, or Professor as he was officially addressed. He was the dean of the department then and sat on the final exam panel. My graduation project was accepted with a good grade and the panel was the final hurdle before I could get my masters degree. It was comrade Niemand's turn to question me. He gave me a nasty, tricky puzzle to solve. I wriggled and tried, but could not come up with the proper answer. This went on for a while; the other professors were rolling their eyes. I thought I was finished. Then the deputy dean, a highly respected and accomplished scientist, turned to Niemand and said,

> "Professor, I wonder, when will you let up? And when you do I would like to have the chance to finish the examination of Mr. Sonnenberg myself, please."

I passed in spite of the commissar, who obviously tried to destroy me out of sheer maliciousness. The others stood up to him, and I was now ready to enter real life. The regime exerted the right to order any graduate to accept a position in any place chosen by the state, and that was called "An order to work." This was significant, for it emphasized that every citizen was the property of the state, to be used as the Party saw fit, especially in my case where I had been on a scholarship throughout my studies. Other students who did not have scholarships, but did not pay tuition—education was free once you were admitted— were also treated the same. There was no other way, free education, but loss of freedom. They tried to send me to the boondocks, and here Mrs. Falkowska came to my rescue. She arranged a meeting with her friend the Minister of Industry, and an interview was arranged at the Aviation Institute in Warsaw. This was the place of my dreams. The interviewer was Prof. Fishdon, my enemy No. 2 in college and the only one I had beside the commissar; otherwise I was in superb standing with all the others. Prof. Fishdon was the science director of the Institute.

"Mr. Sonnenberg, an order came from above to give you a job at the Institute. This is against my better judgment. This is a highly prestigious scientific institution and we accept only the best."

"Sir, who was better than I, in my class?"

"Mr. Lopucha for example, straight As."

"That is true, was there anyone else?"

"We will not have a bidding game here. I have an opening in the prototype department under Dr. Soltyk."

"But Sir, this is not the specialty I was trained in."

"That is the only thing I can offer you, take it or leave it. I have fulfilled the request from above."

In that way I landed in Tadeus Soltyk's operation. He was a prominent and powerful figure in Polish aeronautics, a tall fierce-looking man with an aristocratic bearing and piercing blue eyes, very aloof. He was a descendant of the notorious class of Polish nobles—not an aristocrat though. He was an anticommunist and an anti-Semite of old, views he expressed in jokes and stories to his inner circle of adjutants. I learned that later when I became one of them. Initially, I could only guess from his bearing, I had an eye for that. He reconciled his anticommunism and his service to the regime by invoking his patriotism, which was a mental game many played:

> "Colleague So (that is how he began to address me), our patriotic duty is to work for the Fatherland, it happens to be socialist now and we have to give it our best."

He got away with all this unchallenged, because he had a certain degree of fame and some international connections, and since most of the prewar technical elite had been wiped out there were few competent people left to do the work. Besides, Poland's culture had more of a western tradition as opposed to the Byzantine Russian culture, and it was difficult to turn things around on a dime. As a result some time non-conformism was tolerated in Poland much more than anywhere else in the Soviet block in any case. Poland was called the best barrack in the Soviet concentration camp.

My workstation was put close to Prof. Soltyk's office window, with my back to it. Often I would feel uneasy and look behind me and there he was, standing and staring at my drawing board. At that time he never addressed me directly; if he did not like something I was doing, he would let it be known through my supervisor. The guy I took day-to-day instructions from was a technician, Bruno Biernacki. This was a humiliating situation for a master's degree fellow, right at the bottom of the ladder, way below the supervisor of the section, but then every newly arrived college graduate went through the same. After slaving like this for Bruno for a while I was called into Soltyk's office. This was always nerve-wracking, because one never knew what crime one had committed:

> "Take a seat Colleague So. You are hereby appointed Section Chief, and all paperwork will be adjusted accordingly. I do not think it is necessary to explain your responsibilities, you should know them by now. This is effective as of tomorrow morning; I wish you success, that is all."

"Thank You, Sir."

This is how I entered the Professor's inner circle, and slowly got to know the man. From him I started receiving my leadership training of the highest class and quality. Training that served me well for a lifetime in many different situations, especially in America. In dicey situations I would always ask myself "How would Soltyk handle this one?" Not long into my tenure as chief an opening became available in my specialty, and after being wooed a little I applied. Soltyk called me in and said,

> "Colleague So, I am asking you not to leave. I am not promising anything to you, only a piece of glory, which is sure to come."

I stayed, and my real bond with Soltyk began. The "piece of glory" came much later but it came. I ignored his anti-Semitic stories and jokes. Often one of the lieutenants, and it was usually Winiarski who would say,

> "Doctor, you should be ashamed of yourself saying things like that."

His face would become red then and he would fall silent. But when the next opportunity came along he could not help himself. He was a demanding boss, consummately fair, a model leader. He would grudgingly praise and reward good and imaginative work; praise from him was more valued than from anybody else. He was fiercely protective of all of his people regarding the outside world, though he could be abusive to someone he did not respect. But that was all internal and such persons did not last long in his operation anyway. I remember one of his many outbursts. After the routine morning inspection he stopped at the department he was particularly displeased with that day and shouted out loud,

> "I can see that if I took a troop of monkeys and gave them your task they would do a much better job."

Because of his power he was able to shelter us from the stupid disciplinary actions that had political overtones, and I got the benefit of that once or twice. He generated a mixture of respect and fear; the people working for him were considered by others to be in hell. The hell-dwellers, however, felt a strong bond and loyalty to this man. I became the boss of a section with challenging, enormously interesting and diverse tasks. The people in that particular group were highly individualistic and unruly. If there was an irreconcilable problem with a valuable but difficult employee elsewhere, he was transferred to me. Bruno became the spokesman for that bunch.

"Chief, I need to talk to you, can we go someplace quiet."

They were sometimes irreverent toward the other bosses and played practical jokes on employees outside our group. Another boss would drag me into Soltyks' office to hear complaints about the behavior of my people. The big man listened, and the most he ever said was,

"I hear you; I will take this under consideration.

Now go back to your duties."

He never did anything about it; he simply ignored it. The excellent performance of my team was more important to him, and he did not want to upset the balance that he knew existed in my department. Each of the guys had specific talents, but had been viewed as prima donnas wherever they worked before coming to my section. I grew increasingly fond of my unruly guys. They reciprocated with absolute loyalty to me, and when I had to issue a difficult or controversial order the answer usually was,

"For you chief, it will be done."

One of the other bosses was the big man's brother. His department had occasional design mishaps, which were serious because human lives were at stake. When this occurred Soltyk used to crack his office door open just when people were leaving for home and shout "Witold, come here." Some of my guys pretended that they still had some work to do and lingered around. The next day they would gleefully give me a detailed report of the brutal dressing down Witold received; they had heard every word of Soltyk's loud shouting.

I remember the years under Soltyk with great fondness. One might be surprised at that, but never did I see him discriminate in practice against anybody on the basis of race or gender. In fact he did not tolerate any unfairness and his anti-Semitism appeared to be something odd and ill fitting. It was like a genetic inheritance poking through his skin. When in 1968 I called to bid him my farewell he said,

> "I am very saddened by what has happened and worried for Poland. I understand why you have to leave. Poland is the big loser; I wish you the best of luck"

We all graduated, the four of us, the Kolkhoz, Joe Lewalski, Adam Borowski, Peter Krol and I. During our college years we had been a close-knit family. Now a strange thing started happening. A split started to emerge; Joe and I desperately tried to distance ourselves from anything political as we developed an understanding of the criminal nature of the regime and our rage grew by the day. We started dreaming about leaving communism. Peter on the other had accepted and took an active part in the so-called "renaissance" of the communist movement. Our old friendship prevented us from hating each other but our ties loosened and whenever we met we had sharp exchanges. Peter deteriorated to the point where he boasted that he had trained Arab guerillas against Israel. We inquired about him from time to time, but became estranged. To top it off, he went to Cuba for some work, and when Che Guevara was killed (we were told) he sobbed uncontrollably. Peter died at age 54 of a liver ailment. Adam, the least exited about any politics, married Wanda, a cute little thing who took total control of him. She eventually managed to push him in two mutually exclusive directions. One was the church—for the salvation of his soul, the other the Party—for the advancement of his career. She accomplished both, which was now sort of tolerated as long as he did not parade his church going and kept it quiet. We met once or twice, to find Adam comfortable in the communist "renaissance" atmosphere. Joe and I were outraged and bewildered. We could not understand what had happened, we had been one group for so long, and Joe and I searched for explanations. The best we could come up with was that our genetic heritage had come through and taken hold of our minds and souls. Joe's father was of the bourgeois class (Joe was hiding that more successfully than I) and so was mine. We stopped at that, but then it did not explain Roman Ptak, who was of pure proletarian heritage. Oh... well, there are exceptions to everything! Adam died at the age of 56 from a brain hemorrhage, presumably from smoking since he was a chain smoker.

Joe escaped from Poland and communism in 1972, four years after I did. He came to Canada first and then went to the USA. We are in close contact. He and his wife Eva live in Nevada and became successful under capitalism. When I met Joe at the bus station in Springfield, Ohio we hugged and stood laughing hysterically; the people around us wondered if we had gone mad. Joe said,

> "If they grab me now and put me in chains and drag me to Siberia, I would laugh in their faces all the way, I have fooled them."

I should backtrack a bit to the post-1957 years when the second Jewish exodus out of Poland took place. My friends from the orphanage, Bronek Cyngiser, Jerry Frydman, Akiwa Brand, Jerry Rosner and many others had left for Israel, all having had unspeakably horrible experiences during the war. This exodus was possible because of the turmoil still reverberating in the Soviet block after Stalin's death and the Khrushev speech. Gomulka the somewhat dissident communist became the virtual ruler of Poland in 1956 and a period of relaxation that was called the "Thaw" ensued. Nevertheless anti-Semitism under the guise of anti-imperialism and anti-Zionism became a sanctioned attitude and the long-suppressed national pastime burst into the open, unstoppable. People of Jewish heritage were losing their positions and jobs; the situation became ugly for us wherever we turned. Gomulka who had a Jewish wife, tried to hold back the tide a bit, but in spite of his virtual dictatorial powers he could not. Our deliberations, and those of our friends were soul wrenching. Many of us had built some beginnings of a new life. Bronek was a lieutenant in the Air Force, Frydman a university professor of mathematics, and so on. I was in a quandary too. I had had enough of Poland and communism. Promises had been made that all the horrible stuff that occurred in the past was an aberration and things would be right from now on, but nobody believed that. I wanted out, but my wife Cynthia was still in college and a Polish girl. How could I take her to Israel where she could possibly be subjected to ostracism? I also had qualms of conscience about leaving right after receiving a free education, and I was frightened of the unknown; the capitalist world had been painted so darkly all those years. There was still a very small residue of propaganda left in me, or perhaps it was ignorance. I did not leave with my friends. With a heavy heart and sinking feeling I said farewell to everyone; it was like losing family members one by one. They left mostly from the Milstein flat, which I had inherited. Since they lived in different cities they stayed with me to complete their final preparations for the departure and from my place they left for the railway station. That was an ironic epitaph for comrade Milstein.

THEY LEFT

Bronek Cyngiser

Jerry Frydman

THEY STAYED

Jacob Gutenbaum

Sylvia, my sister

Not everyone left. Some of us, Jacob Guttenbaum, my sister Sylvia and I, for example had a protective shell of decent people around us. Sylvia was studying in Moscow. She, by fudging her application, somehow got in. This was just in the middle of it (1954-1959). She graduated from the Moscow Institute for Farm Machinery & Automobiles with a master's degree. Another kid from the orphanage who got an education. Within the circles around us, we could work and live. Not many such places were left. There was just anguish for us Jews. Soltyk and the people around him created a protective layer for me, beyond which I did not dare to venture. My work for Soltyk resulted in my receiving a National Award for outstanding technical achievement in 1963 together with those in his closest circle. Right after receiving it, I embarked on a campaign to get a decent place to live. We longed for something more reasonable for the three of us than that one-room place. Apartments were allocated by the city authorities; there was no other way for the average working person to get an apartment. I thought I had a strong case. An important engineer, the winner of a national prize, needing working space to further the development of the Socialist State. I finally reached a deputy of one of the Ministries, a Jew, one of the small handful remaining in any capacity.

> "Mister Sonnenberg, I have reviewed your application and I understand your need and sympathize with you, but I cannot grant your request. My position is so precarious here, at the Ministry, that if I give you that apartment, I will be accused of favoring my fellow Jews. Sorry."

We had come full circle back to the years before 1939.

One is tempted to describe the economic living conditions under that system. This though has been belabored in numerous publications and it would become a boring repetition. However, I need to make some brief remarks for readers who might get too enthusiastic about the free education I received. Such an education, by the way, is not uncommon right here under your noses, under "cruel" Capitalism. A friend's son, because of his talent and hard work, got a doctorate from one of the best universities in the USA. The poorest of immigrants, thanks to his ability, he managed to study for free all the way. He now holds a professorship at Duke.

So, here we were, Elizabeth and I working, two salaries, mine not a low according to the standards of the day. No savings though, every penny spent on living expenses, paid out in the long queues for bread and essentials. After work I would rush to one line for bread and Elizabeth to another. I came out from under communism absolutely destitute, anguished for the safety of my family and barely having escaped the corruption of my soul and mind. Communism was so effective at this with so many! I know that the education I received will be pointed to. I paid a prohibitive price for that, figuratively and in financial terms, working for eleven years at far below minimum wage, by international standards. Only the technical education counts anyway, the rest was garbage out from under which I had to dig myself with great effort. Here is a story that was told at the time: an old lady comes into the store and asks for a pound of sausage. The clerk says,

"Madam, this store has no bread."

"But I didn't ask for bread, I asked for sausage!"

I'm sorry, this store has no bread. You will have to go across the street if you want the store that has no sausage."

All the money left over went for health. If our three-year-old Jack got sick, and that was often, we had to seek out doctors in private practice, for it was simply life threatening to go near the UNIVERSAL FREE NATIONAL HEALTH CARE SYSTEM. Same with dentists, and our teeth were in ruin from war and post-war malnutrition. One of the most annoying situations was our cramped living quarters, with not the least prospect for any betterment, a dreary existence and a drearier future. And that was twenty years after the war ended! No wonder people would commit dubious or immoral and degrading deeds to ingratiate themselves to the political elite in order to become a little bit more equal than others. It should to be noted that the top Communist leadership, when sick, went to Sweden for treatment; they knew that their precious lives were in danger from their very own STATE RUN, FREE HEALTH CARE SYSTEM for the masses. The effect of all those problems were dulled for a while during the euphoric years with Soltyk and my beloved aeronautics, but those were coming to an end too, not only because of the political situation in Poland, but because of the simple neglect of the industry. The leadership had other worries, the system was falling apart at the seams and the cracks leading to the fall of the Berlin wall were widening.

My dream of leaving Poland and its cursed communism became an obsession. Elizabeth, who had inherited strong anticommunist feelings from her family (which unfortunately also had a strong anti-Semitic tradition) clearly saw the need too. We started dreaming of nothing else but how to get out. Even though this was an excruciating issue for Elizabeth, mostly because she was attached to her mother. Leaving behind everything, every bit that was familiar, in order to sail into the unknown without knowing any foreign language nor having been exposed to anything but Polish culture, was hard. The decision had been made though; we had to continue our hushed lives, waiting for an opportunity. The opportunity came in 1967-68. In June 1967 the six-day war broke out between Israel and the Arab states. The Polish nation went into fits of schizophrenia. On one hand they could have not been more delighted that "Our Jews had beaten the shit out of the Soviet Arabs," on the other was the anti-Semitism. In every restaurant, at private receptions there were requests for bands to play Jewish songs and music. There was an emotional outpouring of support for Israel, a fit of defiance against the official policy of condemnation of imperialistic Israel. The Party and government responded with equal fervor and outright hysteria (Joe after reading this told me that at the time he counted the words Zionist or Zionistic 84 times on the front page of the then official Party daily

Trybuna Ludu). The anti-Semitic fervor shifted openly to Party and government institutions. The people who in the evening toasted Israel and sang Jewish songs in a half drunken stupor were forced to go to anti-Zionist rallies the next morning. The darkest elements in Polish society took over and there were plenty of them, encouraged by officialdom. The Jews were openly declared traitors to communism and accused of having divided loyalties at best. The famous (in Poland) Polish poet of Jewish heritage Antoni Slonimski (1895-1976) said,

"I understand that one has to have only one Fatherland, but why Egypt?"

The anti Jewish fervor rose to a high pitch. People of Jewish heritage or those suspected of having Jewish background were thrown out of work left and right. There were cases where people were thrown out of emergency rooms after having a heart attack when it was learned that they were Jews. An especially dangerous time came during one of the Party congresses. The Party mob called for blood and shouts were heard " Let's go and finish those bastards off!" We were contemplating asking Elizabeth's Polish friends to put our family up for a night or two, just as people did during the Nazi occupation so they could not be found. Gomulka tried to defuse the situation by declaring,

"Comrades, let the traitors of our sacred cause go, we do not want them in our midst. One must have only one Fatherland [see above-Slonimski] those who are loyal and want to stay can stay."

Since Gomulkas' word was still law in all of Poland this had the effect of setting in motion the opening of the gates. Jews rushed through the obstacle course of scores of bureaucratic requirements that had to be fulfilled if they were to be allowed to leave Poland—handing over their apartments, getting security clearance to leave and so on and so forth, dozens of seals and stamps. The word was out that those with security clearance had to wait for two years and I had security clearance while with Soltyk. Scared, I quit my position, went to the adjacent Aviation Institute and asked if there were any openings where no security clearance was required. I was directed to Mr. Harazny, chief of the Rocket Department. It seemed odd, but Mr. Harazny assured me that there were no secrets. His department built and experimented with weather monitoring rocketry and he would be happy to have me. I started work in a nice room with flowerpots on the window shelf, all by myself, and began marking time while getting all the necessary personal matters in order, in preparation for quitting Poland. Of course that was kept secret and only the closest friends and family knew of my intentions. After a short time I felt that something was not right. The people in the lunch canteen stared at me and most avoided contact. Very soon I found out why. I was summoned to a session of the local Party executive; the luminaries were all there, sitting along the walls on both sides. I came in and stood not far from the door with the comrades on my left and right:

"We asked you to come in to discuss a serious development." (Suspense)

"What is it?

"The people of the Institute are concerned that a Jew is working in a sensitive place like the Rocket Department. Of course, we think it is O.K., but we cannot ignore the concern of the people and their will. We will have to transfer you elsewhere."
"Where to?"

 "To the general test facility. Unless we hear something from you here, in the presence of all the comrades representing the departments, something reassuring, and then we might correct the situation."

This was an invitation to make a teary declaration of loyalty (more on that later).

> "Well, if you think you can correct it then do it, I have nothing to say to you, comrades."

I turned around and went straight to Harazny,

> "Sir, I think I have to quit the Institute, effective immediately. I thank you for your kindness and for having had the courage to give me this job."
>
> "Mr. Sonnenberg, I am terribly ashamed of what has happened. I have tried to do my best to explain that there is nothing that would prevent you from working here. Please, remember that not all the people of the Institute are bad."
>
> "I know that and will remember, thank you again and farewell."

After that I could not find another job for the interim, there were no jobs for Jews. Finally I met Mr. Szymanski, a director of an automotive design bureau, who took me into his outfit. He used to come for a chat, and among other things he said,

> "Mr. Sonnenberg, I must tell you that I am no communist. Although I am in the Party, I hate them."

Another time:

> "I had a Jewish girlfriend, I wanted to marry
> her, but my parents would not allow it. I am
> now approaching retirement and I still
> cannot forget her."

On learning that I was going to Israel,

> "I envy you; I wish I could go with you."

One time there was overtime work, and nobody could stay
but me. Mr. Szymanski said, "I am sorry, the bastards
forbade me to leave a Jew alone on the premises.

I have remembered Mr. Szymanski all these years. I
wish something could be done so that he is not lost to
memory, for he was an outstanding and courageous man.

A number of Jews rushed to declare their loyalty or
were called to do so. One guy went before a panel of
inquisitors and said,

> "Comrades, if I refuse to declare my loyalty you
> will throw me out, and if I do, you will still throw
> me out. Therefore, I propose that you kiss my ass.
> You can take turns if you like."

I thought that the ones who agreed to go through
this were the most despicable wretched beings there could
be. There were a number of those to be found though.

Among other things I had to do was stand before the regional military board to clear away the paperwork for permission to leave. They made a spectacle out of it, a full panel of bemedaled colonels and majors sitting around me in a semicircle and passing questions from one to the other.

"So, lieutenant (I was a lieutenant in the air force reserves), you are leaving us and going to Israel?

"Yes Sir."

"What commission did the imperialists promise you, captain or maybe major? How much money is waiting for you?"

"I do not know of any, sir."

"We have educated you, taken care of you and now you are going to serve our enemies, is that so?"

"Sir, I have worked all those favors off. Twelve years, and some of it brought in hard currency."

I had worked in Indonesia, and they robbed me of half my dollar salary. I wanted to defect then, but Elizabeth, the love of my life, was trapped in Poland. Anyway, my stupid conscience was clear now of even the slightest hang-up.

"So it looks like it is not worth educating you people, not at all."

"Yes, sir that is right."

"If it were not for comrade Gomulka's directive we would show the likes of you your proper place, dismissed."

That directive from Gomulka was the best thing he ever did for us, in spite of the terrible sound of it.

I went to the American embassy and asked if America would be so generous as to accept me, a lesser official greeted me and ushered into the proconsul's office. I showed my papers, confessed all my past sins and after a few questions they went out of the room to deliberate. The proconsul came back after a while and said,

"You will be accepted, get out of Poland immediately, tomorrow if possible."

And so I joined the third post-war Jewish exodus from Poland. This is how freedom for us began, difficult at first, but a condition I have always subconsciously yearned for, and now I experienced it for the first time in my life. The beginning was difficult. My broken English did not help, Elizabeth cried non-stop from nostalgia for her family. I was worried about how it would all work out in this capitalist world, but my chest was bursting with pride that I had had the strength to break away, the feeling of freedom was as tangible as if I had come out from a choking, smoke-filled area into crystal clean fresh air. Elizabeth at some risk, after some time in the US, went back to Poland for a two-week visit to see her mother. She came back and said,

> "I could not have waited another day to come back, how could I have ever lived there?"

She was completely cured of any nostalgia for her homeland, and she flaunted her pride at becoming a US citizen every time she went back to see her family and friends.

Not every Jew left Poland at that time, in 1968. Some of the elderly who had spent their lives in the Party or were too frightened to start life anew in a totally unfamiliar society remained in Poland. Jacob, whom I considered a close friend, stayed. I tried very hard to convince him to leave with me. Mainly for selfish reasons; I thought it would be so much easier if we had each other's support. But Jacob would not budge. His answer was,

> "I am mentally too exhausted to start from scratch in a foreign land."

Jacob was a survivor of the Warsaw ghetto uprising and of Buchenwald. The name Auschwitz is well known, but Buchenwald was equally horrible. He went through hell in both places. He was of diminutive stature, had typical Jewish facial features and limped from polio. While in school, after the war and everywhere else he had a rough time. Harassment of a Jew in the street or other public place could occur anytime and was a sport. Jacob was courageous and in spite of his small size never did allow anyone to get the better of him. In social settings he was always the life of the party, and at work he made friends, which allowed him to endure. He decided to stay, although he did recognize the need to leave. Not everybody was so honest with themselves. I heard rationalizations, which sounded false and painfully stupid,

"One does not abandon a mother only because she is bad."

Mother supposedly being Poland.

In 1992, after the fall of communism, I visited Jacob. In the intervening years Jacob had kept his position at the Institute, he worked and prospered modestly protected by his friends. He was universally liked and a very social and witty person. I went up to his family room's large window. It looked out onto the blank wall of the next apartment building and there I saw a large graffiti across that whole long wall,

"Poland is for Poles only"

Someone must have gone to much trouble to paint that slogan across so big a building. Jacob could see that message every time he opened his curtains. I said,

"Jacob, what is this?"

"Damn it, I have the same right to Poland as those bastards."

That one message made all my worries and struggles in a "foreign" land worthwhile. Poland was never my land and now it really felt very foreign to me. It never earned my allegiance, it was trouble from the moment I became cognizant of my surroundings. The Polish nation had not protected itself or me from the German onslaught. The argument I would hear was that other nations crumbled too. That is a very poor argument. Poland had known for ages that Germany was an enemy coveting its territory; it had repeatedly invaded Poland and tried to annihilate Polish culture. There are no adequate words to describe the obsolescence of the military equipment Poland had and its leadership— all heroism and lack of foresight. The Poles were well aware of the German danger. There was a joke that went around: If a German and a Russian confront a Polish soldier, who does he shoot first? The German, of course—duty before pleasure. It is true that Poland was in an untenable situation between two brutal dictatorships, but this does not erase the neglect of national defense. This is a harsh judgment, but I am not the first to render it.

Under the German occupation substantial elements of the Polish nation behaved devastatingly toward their Jews. The vanquished Dutch and Danes at least made an effort to protect their Jews and often with heroism saved as many as they could. Someone may point to the French and their collaboration with the Germans in many ways including facilitating the German annihilation of French Jewry. That is no excuse for the Poles. P.J. O'Rourke had a good take on the French:

> *"In the meantime I was stuck in Paris. A lot of people get all moist and runny at the mention of this place. I don't get it. It's just a big city no dirtier than most. It does have nice architecture, **because the French chickened out of World War II.** But it is surrounded by the most depressing ring of lower middle class suburbs this side of Smolensk. In fact one working-class neighborhood is named Stalingrad, which goes to show that the French have learned nothing about politics since they*

guillotined all the smart people in 1793."

(O'Rourke, Terror of the Euroweenies)

Besides, Polish culture has never appealed to me. It is full of romanticism and messianism. Their past is futile heroics and tragedy to the point of bringing on tears. The nation has never been united in any endeavor, even in the face of mortal danger; it had a tenacious and destructive class of nobles, which for too long brought disaster after disaster upon the whole nation by their rowdiness and occasional treachery. Never did that nation apply itself to fundamental work in any semblance of unity. The Polish nation has had outstanding personalities and leaders who could never get a following at home. The amazing thing is that these same people were followed in other nations; one has only to mention Kosciusko in the American war of independence. The inescapable conclusion is that —it is Poland and its past mess I have to stay away from, and that is what I mentally have tried to do. Why would anyone persist in clinging to a past that has rejected us, a past punctuated with brutal events for Jews? For those who cling for reasons of emotional attachment I have an explanation, it is the Human Attachment Syndrome discovered by Stalin: Stalin was sitting with his half drunken Politburo cronies around the dinner table in the

Kremlin. He said, "You dummies, all of you, you do not know how to treat people. Bring me a live chicken!" Stalin plucked all the chicken's feathers and the chicken did not run away, it clung to Stalin's boot (he loved wearing boots). "Got the idea?" asked Stalin, looking around the table with his blood-shot evil eyes. One has to be fair to the man and we must credit him with at least one scientific discovery and that a not insignificant one.

In 1992 during my visit to Poland (after the fall of communism) we had a mini- reunion. We went to see Mrs. Falkowska, 86 years old then, in perfect health and lively, witty, very alert, and still, in spite of her age, an attractive lady. We did not immerse ourselves in nostalgia; we talked about contemporary subjects and reviewed all the orphanage children we could remember, their whereabouts and what they were doing. Mrs. Falkowska addressed me with an air of visible disappointment, perhaps hoping for a proper answer,

"Don't you regret now that you left Poland?"

I answered:

"Dear, dear Mrs. Maria, if I hadn't, I would have thrown my life away, and would have lost any traces of self-respect."

That was not very sensitive to those who stayed, but I did not mean to imply a criticism of their decisions. I understood their reasons, and those reasons did not diminish my affection for them. The comment applied strictly to me, and I think they understood it that way.

It is difficult to take a stance on the Polish question. On the one hand there are those dark forces predominating in the Polish nation and its history, on the other there are the outstanding and courageous individuals and a good and many of them. What does one say? My friend Bronek cannot get Poland out his system. It is a longing, which persists despite the terrible things the Poles have done to him, but he cannot forget the good people who saved his life. He does return from Israel to the old places in Poland, barely recognizable now, and talks to the children of those who sheltered him, they themselves being long dead now. He arranged for some of their names to get into Yad Vashem's alley of the righteous. All this is in spite of having succeeded in Israel—after a ferocious struggle to be sure, but he succeeded. He has two sons, both Sabras, and now grandchildren. All are educated and are outstanding people. He has a very close-knit family, a great thing to witness. Such is the case with most who went to Israel or are now scattered around the world

Our mini reunion in 1992. From left to right. Jacob Gutenbaum,Bronek Cyngiser, his wife, Jacob's wife, Mrs Falkowska, Sven

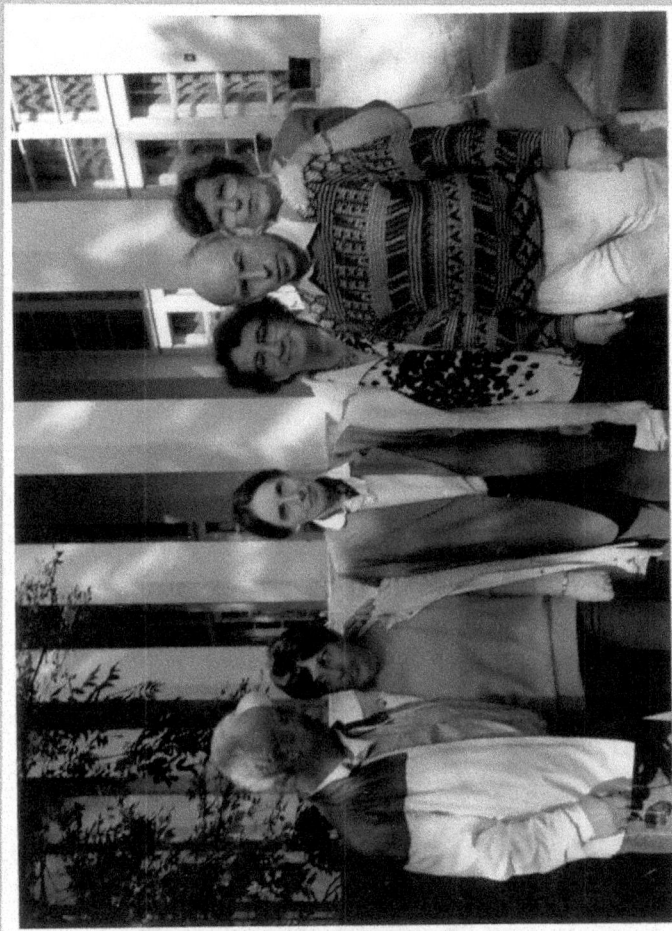

Our mini reunion from left to right

Bronek Cyngiser, his wife Pola, Irene Gutenbaum, Jacob's, wife, Mrs. Falkowska, Sven and Elizabeth, Sven's wife.

Pola Cyngiser, Bronek's wife

Pola, his wife, is younger and was not in Poland
during the war and cannot understand his emotional state. I
can, but I am free from longing for Poland and carry an

indifference with me and that comes out more when reminded. Nevertheless I wish that nation a better fate in the future for all the suffering it has gone through in history. The only thing I guard against is the possibility of doing an injustice to those who were truly heroes, and I try to publicize my gratitude to them for all they have done for me. I have coined a saying,

"A controversial nation, but with many magnificent people in it."

What remains from my Polish experience is a bad taste; however, there is no hatred or consuming feeling of animosity. If I were to define the feeling, then perhaps the closest analogy would be the attitude of an Englishman (I worked with a few for many years)[5]. An English gentleman never hates, he knows that everyone else is an inferior species, what can one expect from the deficient?

---

[5] My editor added his comment here: "The history of England is of course pretty horrible. I enjoy the mid-17 century myself." My comparison to and English attitude or feelings did not imply any general approval of Englishness. It is just one of my observations from having dealt with them over a long stretch of time and it is somewhat fitting.

Nevertheless the lifelong friendships I have made among the Poles remain. Besides Joe and the others already mentioned, from time to time there come to me out of Poland voices of the people I then knew. They remember me and express warm feelings and with nostalgia remind me of things I have done for them, which often I do not remember myself. I cannot dismiss this; it gives me the double satisfaction of knowing that there were such good people around and that I was in their favor.

Would I have left Poland without the events of 1968 to spur me on? Definitely. These events gave me the opportunity and the final push; it was the proverbial last straw for the camel. It was an utterly necessary decision, although laden with fear and apprehension. The residue of years of propaganda about the cruelly competitive conditions under capitalism persisted. I had doubts that I could make it, and more importantly, the responsibility for Elizabeth and Jack weighed heavily. The resolve was absolute. If we had to perish, so be it. No more Poland! To stay would have meant the complete loss of self-respect, and the ability to look at myself in the mirror.

Final Epilogue

Through experience, I have acquired knowledge of the fascist social order and the communist social order. My sequel should probably be titled "Under Capitalism", although the term "under" might be grossly incorrect. I was not "under" anything. I was a free agent living and moving within certain constraints, but those were broad, and the avenues I could travel were so plentiful as to give me the feeling of vast expanses to roam without limits. Empiricism is far superior to any speculative theorizing as was authoritatively confirmed by Colonel Glemp of Smersh/Spectre (007-From Russia with Love). When inspecting the Smersh School of Sabotage she was so right in stating,

"Exercises are good, but there is no substitute for experience."

I have to remind people I meet of that obvious truth, especially the Western intelligentsia, the snotty theoreticians, painfully ignorant.

The moment I stepped onto the American soil another huge burden was lifted. I no longer had to be conscious of my Jewishness, unlike in Poland, or, as I learned, anywhere else. In Poland in any situation, in public places, in offices and at work, I was recognized as a Jew and had to cope with an instant polarization of my surroundings. I went once to the Ministry of Industry on some business for my company. Elizabeth was working there. She came home and asked,

>"Were you in the Ministry Building today?"
>
>"Yes, how do you know?"
>
>"Well, the word spread fast to the fifth floor and to me that a Jew (Zydek-a derogatory term) is in the building. I asked for a description and that is how I guessed."

I was now free of that. Nowhere else in the world is racial profiling so muted, and this applies as well to the black population. Americans would not understand that statement and are sure to disagree with me, but they should check into the fate of blacks that went to the Soviet Union and asked for asylum and freedom from racism—the ultimate in carelessness. That is called ignorance of the world. My long-time friend and employee Habarjan Singh told me that his cousin has just arrived from Germany. I asked how he was doing there. Harry (that is what we called him) said, "The racism is so strong and pervasive that it is not possible for an Indian to live there."

That freedom is now and has been under assault from the intellectual elite here in the USA and worldwide. This is not a supposition anymore, it is the truth and evident every day. One has only to look at the pressure exerted for multiculturalism, which results in constraints within narrow limits, politically correct speech, and prohibition of the free expression of ideas, the frantic effort to fragmentize our society and to recognize and promote the separatism of even the tiniest ethnic or behaviorally different group. Those elite had changed its mantle; they hated capitalism all along and strove to destroy it. With communism gone, they will not let go of their dreams of an ideal society where the lamb lies down with the lion in peace and everyone is **betrizeized** [4].

During the communist era they, the intellectual class everywhere in the world, aided and abetted that criminal movement. The mildest form of their support for communism was covering up and thwarting the truth trying to come out or needing to be disseminated. Jean-Paul Sartre (1905-1980) when debating whether to disclose Khrushchev's speech and Soviet atrocities to the French workers said no,

"In order not to throw the workers of Billancout into despair."

One might have hoped that Communism was gone, thrown onto the trash heap of history by the side of a hundred million human beings tortured, and murdered. However, no, although the beautiful, idealistic, and compassionate souls will not invoke the bankrupt name of communism anymore, now they have a myriad other "isms" to push.

The intellectual is a guilt-ridden individual because of his good and secure life in academia or because of the millions he is accumulating in Hollywood and cannot see much beyond his feeling of short sighted compassion, say, Joyce Brown, the notorious street dweller. She returned to the Manhattan Bank entrance after every benevolent offer Mayor Koch could come up with. She evidently got her kicks from watching the CEO's stepping over her territorial markings. Left intellectuals spin out their noble theories from cases similar to this and are constantly busy laboring on schemes to make mankind happy. They have only contempt for those of us who have, by the sweat of their brows, lifted a good portion of humankind out of the dark ages of ignorance and want. They (the lefty intellectual luminaries) have usually messy personal lives and neglected offspring, or are highly corrupt, but run around lecturing others how they MUST live. The more idealistic and pure-hearted moan and worry themselves sick because of AIDS in Africa. It is a cursed class that has brought unmitigated disaster upon humankind. Fascism was the brainchild of the intellectuals—Nietzsche and company. Marxism was also in development by intellectuals of all stripes well before Marx and Engels codified it to become precursors for the practitioners of such fame as Lenin, Stalin, and Mao. What they lack is the courage to machinegun their opponents.[6] For that, they recruit followers from the (by them) befuddled working class or the lumpen-proletariat dregs of society like the the great ones have done (Hitler, Stalin, Pol Pot and company). After the fall of the Soviet Union one of the prominent correspondents of a major Western paper in Moscow said to his revered Russian leaders, now fallen,

"Thanks for having tried."
There was a joke going around when I was still in Poland. It went like this,

---

[6] But come to think of it, they might develop that courage. What then should we do to stop them? In America, I mean.

"What is the proof that communism was not invented by scientists or Engineers?"

"If it was, they would first try it out on monkeys."

There is a distinct group of people that can hardly qualify as intellectuals; I would classify them as wannabes, the likes of Jimmy Carter or Bishop Desmond Tutu. Joe singled those two out, I do not know why or maybe I could guess (Joe Lewalski, my friend, described earlier, now in the US). He has become a virulent anti-liberal, with good reason, of course. Only O'Rourke surpasses him.

A civilized person should no more tolerate the presence of a liberal than the presence of a member of the Klu Klux Klan. Indeed, it may be argued that liberalism is worse than the KKK insofar as Klansmen only hate some people while liberals hate them all. (O'Rourke, Current and Recurrent Events)

So far, I have mentioned some element that is ostensibly all noble cause and good faith. What comes out now is appalling; every day there is another bucket of filth being emptied since with its tales of horrible material corruption (not the biggest worry) of the left and their ruthless drive for power and control over the population. They are relentlessly pushing toward socialism, and the least they would settle for is a bureaucratically controlled society like Canada, where they are sure to become the dictating elite in an "egalitarian" and stagnant society and become much more equal than the "masses".

The above could be considered an emotional outburst. I would plead with the reader to remember that I came out from under fascism with my family destroyed, barely alive and absolutely destitute. I came out from under communism destitute, anguished for the safety of my family and barely having escaped the corruption of my soul and mind. Communism was so effective at this with so many! I know that the education I received will be pointed to. I paid a prohibitive price for that, figuratively and in financial terms, working for eleven years at far below minimum wage, by international standards. Only the technical education counts anyway, the rest was garbage out from under which I had to dig myself with great effort. I also anticipate the argument that the liberal elite forged the present tolerance we experience in America. That is patently false for a number of reasons. If anything they are at work to destroy it now. First, America was always more tolerant than the rest of the world. This is why millions flocked to this shore. Even the blacks with their abject history of slavery were better off here than in Africa. One has to remember the boxing match held in Zaire between the two black boxing heroes at the time. A huge black following went there from the States to watch the spectacle. On returning one of the more perceptive gave this impression of Zaire: "I am glad our forefathers did not miss the boat."

The emancipation of blacks and the diminution of anti-Semitism and whatever tolerance we have now in the US was brought about not by the zealot idealistic left. Decent people brought it about, and the now so much maligned Charleton Heston, without political screams and destructive ideologies. The left or the far left was busy supporting the crumbling Soviet regime and shipping grain and supplies to them, with Carter eventually disclosing his ignorant surprised, "I did not know that they were that evil." Apparently reading the bible every night, in Spanish did not enlighten him much. I believe he was just ignorant.

That could not and should not be said of for example the so-very-respected (in academia, of course) John Kenneth Galbraith, a supposed brilliant economist who was very consistently trying to befuddle the American readership. I could not believe my eyes when I read his article (where else but in the New Yorker) comparing the American economy to the Soviet System. The upshot of that article was that they (the Soviets) had it almost right, a few improvements and they would surpass us, and that was in the mid-seventies. Was he that gullible? Or was it the result of him going on a guided Volga Canal trip, with a pilgrimage to the holy land many American leftists used to make? O'Rourke captured the spirit of one of those trips; although he professed that he became speechless. Nevertheless, he was able to squeeze out a few words. Here is an excerpt from his "Current and Recurrent Events" essay (1995):

. . . .

Being a journalist, 1 had spent most of my career making things up. It was Michael Kinsley who first pointed out to me that the world is funnier than I am. In 1982 Kinsley was the editor of Harper's *magazine (which job he lost-I swear this is true- for not being enough of a pinko sap). Michael gave me an assignment to travel on a Volga River cruise with a group of aging American leftists. Watching this bunch try to put a good face on the butt-end of the Brezhnev years was . . . words fail me. I must resort, as writers will when words fail them, to quoting myself.*

As we were going through the lock of the Don-Volga canal an aging American leftist came nattering up beside me at the rail.

"Isn't it marvelous?" she said, staring at a gigantic blank wall of concrete. "They're such wonderful engineers in the Soviet Union."

I agreed it was an impressive piece of work.

"Marvelous, marvelous, marvelous, marvelous," she said. She peeked over the side. "And where *do* they get all the water?"....

It would be too time-consuming to compile the long list of the many who seemingly worked directly as if on the payroll of the Soviets. The veiled activity of the high-minded intellectual elite of the Galbraith type was far more damaging and insidious.

The intelligent reader with an open mind and without preconceived notions i.e. faith, will hopefully see that the consequence of right wing activity is often fascism and of left wing is communism or its *kin*. I have to invoke here my transposition of the Taguchi Method known in engineering. Taguchi constructed a so-called social loss function whereby any deviation from the optimum specification in either direction plus or minus causes severe social losses. It struck me that the Taguchi curve can also be called the Jewish Loss Function and here is an illustration for it:

The Jewish Loss function

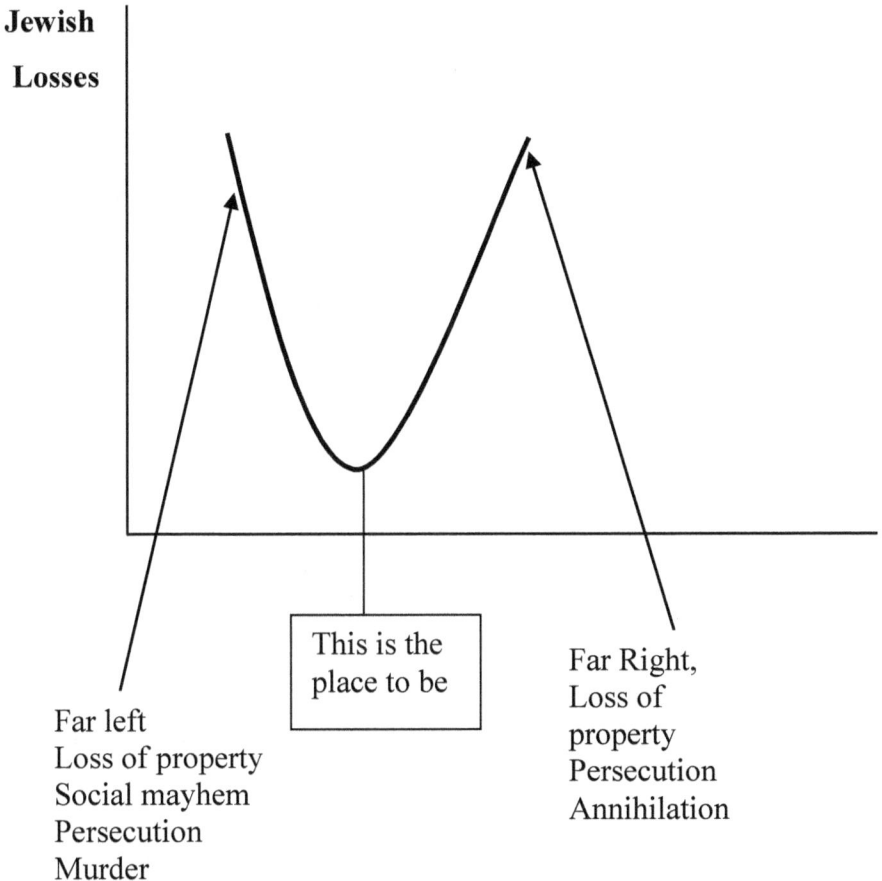

Jewish

Losses

This is the
place to be

Far left
Loss of property
Social mayhem
Persecution
Murder

Far Right,
Loss of
property
Persecution
Annihilation

The restless Jewish mind when applied to science, the arts and economics, has contributed enormously to human progress; it would be superfluous to enumerate all the exhilarating achievement of Jews in the course of human history. Unfortunately, the same mind when applied to social issues produces disaster for the Jews and everyone else. The fatal mixture of shortsighted compassion that immediately overrides reason, combined with smarts and zeal, is most destructive. No historical lesson will change this, "When will they ever learn?" Never, is my answer. That automatic zealous emotional reaction to perceived or real social oppression or injustice of any group of people anywhere causes an automatic sympathetic impulse, engagement and worry. If we had a species of humanoids living on the moon or Mars and in some kind of trouble we would find Jews very concerned about it and starting an emancipation movement.

In the Soviets, if Stalin had not died in time very much overdue, they (the beautiful souls) would have surely brought another holocaust upon all Jews. Plans were ready to round up all Jews and send them to gulags or the infested region in Siberia called Birobidjan. That was the result of the endgame of communism to which too many Jews have contributed by their brilliant social "engineering" skills (*what a horribly blasphemous misapplication of a term!*). In the USA they have gotten the eternal gratitude of Louis Farrakhan for their struggle for Negro emancipation and so on and so forth. Why are those socially conscious Jews not minding their own business? The answer is that through the ages the Jews were severely persecuted almost everywhere and chased from place to place in the Diaspora. That has created a genetic shift—a propensity for compassion (*deep awareness of the suffering of another coupled with the wish to relieve it.*). It is so nonsensical at times, that one cringes. My friend Bronek when visiting me here in the USA got into a fight with another visitor in my house at the time, a New York Jew. The New Yorker stated that he sympathizes with the Palestinians; the death toll is disproportionately high for them as opposed to the Israelis. Bronek, who is the gentlest person in the world, was ready to hit him.

There are some hopeful signs on the horizon, but not enough. A few Jews here in the USA of some prominence, seem to understand the problem and are fighting to bring us in line with Taguchi. I will mention some names here; these are the Cristol family, David Horowitz, Ben Wattenberg, William Safire and some others.

I feel great discomfort for not having the aptitude to join those and make a difference. I am a lifelong engineer, and that has put me in the position of a helpless spectator of events and a helpless victim of the handiwork of the compassionate "brilliant" social manipulators. Our disastrous condition is that they always seem to find enough gullible souls to exercise their brilliance upon.

It is the proper place to include part of a Glenn Beck interview with David Horowitz.

. . . .

BECK: The hate.

HOROWITZ: What it comes from is a vision of a possible future that is perfect — where there is no racism, no sexism, no war, no poverty. Where there's social justice instead. If you believe that you can achieve a world like that then you see yourself in effect as part of the Army of the Saints, and everybody opposing you is the Party of Satan. If you think of hellfire and damnation preachers you understand exactly who "liberals" are.

BECK: You see it in Al Gore.

HOROWITZ: Of course.

BECK: You see it in anybody who's on this climate thing. If you disagree with them you're going directly to hell.

HOROWITZ: Exactly. Where does all this secular crusading come from? If you look at the decline of the organized religions which begins around the time of Darwin, that's when you have the rise of socialism,

Communism, fascism, all secular chiliastic faiths. All of these secularisms are really searches for redemption. But redemption in this life and achieved by human beings.

BECK: This is where President Obama gets the idea of collective salvation that he is always preaching about, which is the exact opposite of the Christian idea. The exact opposite understanding of what Christ, a divine being, did.

HOROWITZ: Exactly.

BECK: There is no collective salvation.

HOROWITZ: The one addition you have to make to this analysis, is to include the Islamists who are not secular but who believe in redeeming this world. A true Christian or Jew understands that only God can make this world right. The first chapters of Genesis reflect a very profound understanding of who we are.

When God expelled us from the Garden of Eden he put an angel with a flaming sword at the gate to prevent us from returning. We are the problem, not society. Society is just a reflection of who we are. We are the problem, and we can't fix it. If you understand that, then you are a conservative. If you think that the human problem can be fixed by other human beings then you're a leftist and dangerous.

....

References

(1) a. Modern Times by Paul Johnson – The High Noon
Aggression Chapter.

Harper & Row Publishers, 1985

b. **http://www.hitlerstoppedbyfranco.com/jews/**.
We have been taught that General Franco was a friend of
Adolph Hitler and consequently an anti-Semite. Our
teacher: The world's most successful Defamation League,
Soviet Russia's Comintern (Communist International).
Why? Because General Franco, by winning the Spanish
Civil War ended the Soviet presence in Spain and thwarted
Russia's hopes to make Spain another Iron Curtain country.
So, ignoring the fact that Franco's ancestors were
Marranos, Spanish Jews who converted to Christianity
during the middle Ages under threat of death or
persecution, here is testimony from non-interested parties:
**FRANCISCOFRANCO, BENEFACTOR OF THE
JEWS:**
However general history may judge him, in Jewish history,
he shall certainly occupy a special place...Jews should
honor and bless the memory of this great benefactor of the
Jewish people...who neither sought nor reaped any benefit
from what he did.

From a four page obituary in *The American Sephardi*
Journal of the Sephardic Studies Program of Yeshiva
University, volume IX, 1978.

James Michner in *Iberia*, 1968, page 547: "...Generalissimo
Franco is highly regarded by Jews; during the worst days of
World War II, when pressures from Hitler were at their
heaviest, Franco refused to issue anti-Jewish edicts and
instead provided a sanctuary, never violated, for Jews who
managed to make it to Spain. Many thousands of Jews owe
their lives to Franco, and this is not forgotten.

In *Resolutions* of the War Emergency Conference of the
World Jewish Congress, Atlantic City, New Jersey,
November 26-30, 1944, page 15: "The War Emergency
Conference extends its gratitude to the Holy See and to the
Governments of Sweden, Switzerland, and Spain... for the
protection they offered under difficult conditions to the
persecuted Jews of Hungary..."

In the *Congressional Record* of January 24, 1950, Rep.
Abraham Multer quotes a spokesman for the Joint
Distribution Committee: "During the height of Hitler's
blood baths, upwards of 60,000 Jews had been saved by the
generosity of Spanish authorities."

Newsweek, March 2, 1970: "...a respected U.S. rabbi has
come forward with surprising evidence that tens of

thousands of Jews were saved from Nazi ovens by the personal intervention of an unlikely protector. Spain's Generalissimo Franco, in so many other respects a wartime collaborator of Adolf Hitler. "I have absolute proof that Franco saved more than 60,000 Jews during World War II, says Rabbi Chaim Lipscitz of Brooklyn's Torah Vodaath and Mesitva rabbinical seminary."

c. For a more detailed treatment of Spain's role during the Holocaust see:

Spain and Jews During the Holocaust by Aaron Haas B.A. Paper The University of Chicago May 2000

(2) a. INTERMARIUM Volume 1, Number 3. The Jewish Pogrom in Kielce, July 1946 - New Evidence. Bozena Szaynok. ...

www.columbia.edu/cu/ece/research/intermarium/interm arium-vol1.html

b. Modern Times, Paul Johnson
Harper & Row Publishers, 1985

c. The illustrated History of the Jewish People
Jane S. Gerber, Oded Irshai et al.

(3) Pavlik Morozov 1918(?)-1932 Copyright © 1999 by Hugo S. Cunningham

> Pavlik Morozov, supposedly killed by "kulak" relatives for denouncing his father to Stalin's secret police (OGPU-NKVD), was adopted as a patron saint by the "Young Pioneers," the Soviet equivalent to the "Boy Scouts." His life exemplified the duty of all good Soviet citizens to become informers, even at the expense of family ties.

> The photo (right) shows a famous statue of Pavlik Morozov, in a park named for him in Moscow, in the Krasnaya Presnya district about 2 kilometers west of the Kremlin. He is holding a flag. When the photo was taken in 1990, the park was immaculately maintained.

(4)   **Betrization** is in the future. It is an inoculation, mandatory like measles shots today, for every newborn child. It is brought about and forced on society by the ever-growing, ever-stronger well-wishers movement and the strong support from feminists to eliminate any violence from society. A betrizeized individual either man or woman, is incapable of any act of violence or of taking any kind of risk where danger is involved. It permanently alters the brain. Robots perform any work involving violence or risk and act explicitly under well-controlled orders from especially appointed human committees. Lovemaking is an activity involving risk and for that, couples drink perto before any engagement. Perto has only a temporary effect and its dispensation to married couples is strictly controlled.

(Stanislaw Lem, Return From The Stars,
Harvest/HBJ Book)

ADDENDUM A

Letter to Joe Lewalski,

Dear Joe,

Thank you very much for such a thorough review of my essay, "Under Communism." I felt an obligation to submit it to you since you were mentioned in it, and if by any chance this is published, you ought to know what I have written about you. The second reason was to check my memory about events and times spent together under that system.

I have incorporated all the corrections and clarifications you suggested. I will now address your "General Remarks" in the order submitted.

1. *Your "heavy duty" resentment and harsh wording toward the end of the narrative is not funny and may turn readers off. It does not compare to O'Rourke, who does the "bitching" in such an interesting way.*

First, it is impossible for me, in my writing, to come close to the talented Mr. O'Rourke, but even if I had the capability, I would not attempt satire or sarcasm, which O'Rourke weaves into his books and essays so brilliantly. Satire or sarcasm tends to be dismissed and not taken seriously, and it often does not find its mark and fails to hurt –"Oh… the guy is just being sarcastic," is the typical reaction. The subject is too serious and too much blood has flowed to make it into a satire. Those who are unable to understand or learn and reflect or acknowledge I want to hurt and hurt badly. Let them not finish my narrative and fume in anger forever.

1. *Your story does not show us in a dramatic way, "as failing heroes"*— failing in…. what, Joe?

I need to remind you here that some of us were in the "fog" only from 1945-46 to 1956, and sometimes a much shorter period, when even the slightest illusion fell away, after the brutal Soviet actions in Hungary. I had an earlier shock related to the "Doctor's affair". Most important, though, was the fact that we never lost our humanity, intellectual honesty and integrity. We never committed an immoral or treacherous act against anybody as countless others did under that regime. We never lost the capability to tell right from wrong even under intense corrosive and corrupting pressures. If anything, we were misled and ignorant as to the true nature of communisms, we did not know their true history (they were hiding it so skillfully). Nevertheless, we did not allow ourselves to be infected with the ruthless and criminal notions communism was so replete with. We did not fail in anything, we just saw through the criminal cabal at some point and it is the slow progress toward that that I was trying to show.

So, to say failing heroes, even perversely, is not appropriate. One could sarcastically say that we were supposed to be in the "Communist Heaven" and have fallen from it, but I listed above the reasons why we were never true "failures," we did not fail, we fell out badly with Communism and its associates.

3. *These days, when I meet a pony tailed, overweight, graying man at a gathering of intellectuals telling me that the Russian Revolution was a noble experiment, I am just sad and do not respond, because if I do, he will give me an all-knowing smile back and say "What is wrong with feeding the children?"*

That is wrong Joe. A vigorous opposition should be given to those ponytails any time there is an opportunity. To me they do not respond with a smile, they become outraged, angry and all worked up. A few of those jolts and they may lose their ponytail; the silent majority has too many times allowed the shrill to have the day. I must remind you about Solshenitzin, who said that when the Bolshevik troikas came to people's homes to haul them away in the middle of the night, those people should have met them with axes, and maybe if they had, there would have been no need for my "heavy duty" resentment. I am not anticipating an all-knowing smile; I usually manage to leave them breathless with rage.

Thank you for reminding me of the Oleksiak story, I will weave it in. At the time it made the rounds in the student community and contributed greatly to the understanding of how evil that Soviet Empire really was.

ADDENDUM B
P J. O'Rourke

The Problem with Communism

Editorial from the 1979 "Politics" Issue

What's there to say about Communism, anyway? I mean, besides that it's bad and don't do any of it. We all know it's bad. It's bad because it's based on unsound socioeconomic premises, has no respect for individual liberty, produces a totalitarian autocracy in every example of its practical applications as a system of government and plenty worse, besides. But that's not why it's really bad. Who cares about all that egghead guff? The real reason that

Communism is bad is because it isn't any fun. It's no kicks, no giggles, no laughs—a nine-inning goose egg in the hoot-and-holler league. And there's a simple reason why that's so. Communism is no fun because of Communists.

Why, your Communist is the type of guy or gal who only cares about great big rights and wrongs—the really tremendous and large ones the size of whole countries and stuff. And there's nothing worse in the world than somebody who cares about rights and wrongs that big.

Now, everybody cares about regular rights and wrongs, rights and wrongs that are about our size. Your wife, for instance just what has she been doing during the day? Do you think that's "wrong"? Would it be "right" to give her a pop in the yap? Everybody cares about rights and wrongs like that. That's only human. That's what keeps us from being like animals and only having rights and wrongs that you have to pee around the boundaries of to get established. Human beings should never have to pee on anything to establish their rights. That's written straight into the US. Constitution, I think, or should be. Incidentally, what your wife's doing is wrong and it's all right to hit her in most states so long as it doesn't leave a mark. But these other rights and wrongs, the really big kind, are a different matter. When people start getting thoughtful about these it just louses them up. That's because if you have a gigantic "right," well, it's just too big to ever really get to see much of. And if you have a huge "wrong," it's just too enormous to ever get it fixed. Whereas little rights and wrongs, the kind normal people like us have, aren't that fancy: I mean, sooner or later the old sow runs off with a Bible salesman or, at worst, you go to jail for a while. But the people who care about the great big rights and wrongs never get them to go away, and this turns these people sad and gloomy.

Not that being sad and gloomy is what makes such people so awful, because some sad and gloomy people— you know, the kind who drink for hours and then suddenly jump up and rip the bar stools out of the floor—are interesting and more or less okay, sometimes. But it's different with the sad and gloomy people who care about big rights and wrongs, which are sad and gloomy and also really drips in spades.

They're whiners and criers, and nothing is ever right so far as they're concerned-somebody's always being persecuted against or exploited on or suffering with something somewhere, and we should all be out doing something about it instead of just having fun, like drinking gin or getting a little leg in the back of your Ford. This is what the Communist-type person says. And look at their countries, such as Russia: no good bands, no dance halls, no racy movies, no spicy magazines, no horse tracks, no burlesque shows—they don't even have modern art (and there is nothing on earth more boring than modern art, but even that's too exciting for them). This comes from having a country-full of Communist-type people—the kind of people who worry about great big rights and wrongs. I'm here to tell you that turns them into dips and limpwicks and weenies. I don't know how it works, exactly, but it does. Maybe thinking about all that big important stuff makes them sit the way they all do, you know, with their legs crossed at the knees and pressed together too hard so that the lower part of their body doesn't get as much blood as it needs so that they don't develop all their sex hormones, which are the hormones that make you want to have a good time, and therefore, they don't want to drink a lot and eat good food and get loved up like we do, but just want to worry instead. Whatever it is, it makes for the kind of person who, when he was a kid, used to do next Tuesday's homework on last Friday night, if you know what I mean. Lots of times he used to be a minister's son, which isn't a Communist, exactly, but usually was a Presbyterian, which is not as bad but still stinks. Well, what you did to the minister's kid was tie him to a fence post with his pants off and dip his pecker in fresh cream and turn a half-weaned calf loose on him. Which is exactly what we ought to do to all the Communists in the world, except with atom bombs.